Eric Begbie

Fowling in the Wild

Adapted from "Fowler in the Wild"

Eric Begbie

Fowling in the Wild

Memories of a Longshore Gunner

Copyright © 2008 Eric Begbie
All Rights Reserved

Other books by Eric Begbie include:
Modern Wildfowling (1980 and 1989)
The Sportsman's Companion (1981)
The New Wildfowler – 3rd Edition (Ed.) (1987)
Fowler in the Wild (1988)
*Gundog Training made Easy (2005)
*Gundog Training for the Duck and Goose Hunter (2006)
*A Waterfowler's Bedside Book (2006)

*also available from www.lulu.com

ISBN 978-1-4092-1853-1

Contents

Introduction 5
The Call of the Estuary 7
Exploring New Foreshores 17
Fowl Weather 29
Inland Interludes 41
Dogs and Guns 53
American Adventures 67
Epilogue 75

4

Introduction

Wildfowling is the pursuit of wild fowl in wild places. As a shooting sport it is unique in that success depends more upon the wildfowler's knowledge of the habits and habitat of his quarry than upon his marksmanship skills. It is, however, more than just a sport. For those of us who have responded to the call of a wild estuary, fowling can become a way of life, a consuming passion which leads us relentlessly to seek a better understanding of the birds which inhabit the land and water beyond the tideline.

In the eyes of many folk, the wildfowler must appear to be a very strange individual. Whether he sets out on a mild October morning, battles against the gale of a November storm or endures frozen fingers in late December, the longshore gunner is privy to a world which is known to only a tiny proportion of 20th-Century mankind. The marshes and saltings below the sea wall, especially in mid-winter, constitute one of the last remaining areas of true wilderness to be found in this crowded country. When the rest of the nation is asleep, a solitary wildfowler can experience a communion with nature which is well-nigh impossible in any other setting.

Not only will he share his world with a rich multitude of genuinely wild fauna, he will encounter weather conditions which would send most of his compatriots scurrying for sanctuary. To be successful at his craft he must learn to read the natural signs - wind, tide and moon - and become thoroughly familiar with the topography of his chosen estuary. Dawn and dusk will become as significant to him as "News at Ten" is to his city-bound brethren.

All the fowler's senses play their part in revealing to him the full wonder of this environment. He sees dark storm clouds scudding across a slowly lightening sky. He hears the ebb and flow of tides and the myriad calling of dozens of species of shore birds. He smells the iodine of estuarine vegetation and tastes the salt spray in the air. All of those combine to fill out the mental images which colour his anticipation as each new season draws nigh and they are all part of the memories which sustain him through the days when his gun is safely locked away in its cupboard.

Each and every wildfowling expedition is an adventure during which new problems arise and new solutions are found. In this way one's knowledge progressively expands with the result that the novice gradually transforms into an accomplished sportsman. There are less-experienced wildfowlers and more-experienced wildfowlers but there are no experts. The span of a human life is too short for any individual to acquire a monopoly of fowling truth; so let the man who thinks that he knows it all put away his thigh boots and take up golf or clay pigeon shooting instead.

It is, therefore, with a sense of humility that this book has been compiled. I have attempted to recount a selection of personal wildfowling tales which I hope will begin to illustrate some of the fundamental principles and practices of the sport. If the accounts of geese flighting over a windswept foreshore serve to fire the imagination of the novice I will be well pleased; should more proficient fowlers feel that they have learned anything new, I shall be delighted.

Much has changed in recent years, especially in terms of the legislation which determines the species which may, or may not, be pursued. Ethics and codes of conduct are also subject to continuous updating as fowlers become increasingly conscious of the need to conserve both quarry and wildfowl habitat. The lead which has been taken by the British Association for Shooting and Conservation is one which must be firmly followed by sportsmen throughout the country.

Chapter 1

The Call of the Estuary

Red and brown. Those were the predominant colours in the eyes of a small boy searching for hermit crabs in a rock pool on the southern shore of the Firth of Forth. The dull red of ancient geological formations interspersed with slippery brown patches of bladder wrack. The collecting urge was strong and the most readily secured prizes were to be found underfoot. Shellfish, sea anemones, starfish and spiny urchins - indeed any creature which could be carried home in a 2lb jam jar half filled with sea water. With a searching gaze constantly directed downwards it was not difficult to imagine that the whole world was red and brown.

Green and blue and yellow were not then serious colours. On happy summer days there were sandy beaches to be enjoyed, lush meadows to be explored and clear skies under which to dream but, when the hunting instinct prevailed, when there was juvenile work to be done, it was back to the red and brown land where so many natural treasures could be picked by merely upturning a few water-covered stones.

The estuary was a major feature of those boyhood years. My parents' house had been built, a century earlier, as the residence for the gaffer of the salt pans and it quite literally rose from the tideline on massive stone buttresses. At first we gained access to the foreshore by means of a rope ladder secured to a rusty iron hook on a downstairs window sill while a pulley fixed to the garden wall allowed driftwood, sand and gravel to be hauled up from the beach in abandoned fish creels. In that age of austerity there was a multitude of uses to which the spoils of the sea could be put.

Then the great day arrived when my father decided to build a permanent fight of steps to replace that fraying, swaying rope ladder. The high water mark was combed for timber to use as shuttering, bucketful upon bucketful of coarse sand and crushed shells was carried along the beach to be hand-mixed with cement and the backbreaking task of creating a concrete staircase began. In the mind of a small boy the rock pools, mussel beds and weed banks had suddenly drawn even closer.

Not that the estuary was always welcoming. When winter storms arrived I would lie awake at night listening fearfully to the waves pounding upon the house walls and to the high spiteful rattle of salt spray being whipped against my bedroom window. There was no double glazing in those days. Even thick wooden shutters and heavy curtains could do little to deaden the noise of a tempest raging without.

In the morning different sounds might be heard. Should the gale have abated a little, I would be wakened by the plaintive calling of gulls wheeling over the shore. Driven in from the North Sea by the foulest of weather, they would find rich pickings amongst the limpets and periwinkles which had been torn from their rocky havens by the storm. Bounty of another sort would also be washed up by the succeeding tides. Fishboxes, baskets, nets and floats of cork or glass littered the tideline and had to be assiduously gathered in case - just in case - they might be of some future utility.

Little did I realise that in later years I would crave to be out on the foreshore whenever conditions turned wild and dirty; that a different kind of harvest could be yielded by the estuary.

During the succeeding few summers the world expanded and its horizon lifted beyond the immediate red and brown. So too did the range of produce which could be culled from the shore. When the tide was at full ebb, a mussel might be scooped from its shell, tied to the end of a fathom length of twine and dangled from the farthest rocky outcrops as bait for partans - the huge edible crabs which could crush a carelessly placed finger between their powerful pincers. The thrill was in the capture of those great crustaceans and they were always released unharmed to scuttle back to their underwater caverns. My grandmother's insistence that partans could be cooked only by dropping them alive into a pot of boiling water served to ensure that none were taken home to meet such a fate.

The acquisition of a fishing line brought further quarry within reach. At first one was satisfied with poodlies and sprats but, before long, mackerel and flounders were sought with increasing avidity and, at last, the hunting instinct was rewarded with food for the table.

It was about that time that the boy became aware that birds other than gulls frequented the estuary. In autumn, turnstones searched the dried seaweed at high water mark for sandhoppers while, after the tide receded to expose great flats of mud and sand, piping trips of dunlin and knot would wheel in to feed on molluscs or worms. With winter's approach the waders were joined by larger fowl - sea duck riding out the waves in rafts up to ten thousand strong and skeins of wild geese which passed high overhead at dawn and dusk.

One day my father arrived home with an old astronomical telescope - 48 inches of solid brass casing, lenses like saucers and a tripod upon which the whole apparatus perched. Before long the novelty of scanning the heavens wore off so the telescope gained a permanent position at an upstairs window from which the foreshore and waters of the estuary might be examined. With the aid of those powerful optics the flocks of anonymous duck could be identified as scaup, eider, goldeneye or scoter and the less common arrivals of longtails, merganser, wigeon or shelduck were noted carefully in an exercise book from which the wasted pages of arithmetic or grammar had been carefully torn.

When the years of primary education drew to a close I had to travel daily into the city for schooling and my attention to birds became wider and progressively more scientific. Natural history society field expeditions introduced the wildlife of wood, meadow and moorland while biology lessons provided a systematic understanding of ecology and behaviour. Throughout that time, however, the birds of the estuary were not forgotten and, at every opportunity, the foreshore was revisited.

The history of wildfowling contains many accounts of personal transitions between fowler and naturalist. By no means is this a one-way phenomenon and, for every accomplished ornithologist whose interest in birds stemmed from days spent with gun and dog, there is a wildfowler who can claim that his love of the sport developed from a birdwatching apprenticeship. It would beg criticism to suggest too emphatically that no naturalist can truly understand the habits of wildfowl unless he has hunted them on our wild coastal marshes but there can be little doubt that few hobbyist twitchers share the awe and respect with which the longshore gunner regards his quarry. Eyebrows are less likely to be raised at the assertion that no wildfowler can enjoy the fullness of his pursuit without a keen knowledge of the habits and habitat of the more common duck and goose species.

During my own adolescent years the hunting urge was largely fulfilled by fishing for trout in the rivers of East Lothian while my response to the call of the estuary lay in field expeditions with binoculars and notebook. The lure of the saltings cannot be readily assuaged, however, by sitting at the roadside scanning the marsh from afar and it was not long before flooded gutters were being crossed and muddy creeks followed in an attempt to attain a closer encounter with the fowl. Even then there were limits to the degree of satisfaction which could be derived from studying birds while they roosted or preened during the daylight hours so, gradually, just as I had forsaken the civilised stances from which my contemporaries watched wildfowl, I also forsook the civilised times of day during which they ticked off their species lists. Instead of wandering down to the shore, dressed in short-sleeved shirt and flannels on a summer's afternoon, I might be found crawling about a frozen marsh before dawn in midwinter. Only then could the primordial thrill of sharing a desolate landscape with flighting pinkfooted geese be fully experienced.

It was on such a cold December morning that fate conspired to introduce me to the world of wildfowling. For a few days it had been rumoured that two bean geese were associating with the pinkfeet on the estuary and I could hardly wait for the weekend to mount an attempt at spotting those rare birds. Only a couple of hundred bean geese migrate regularly to Britain and those normally spend the winter split between the Yare marshes in Norfolk and Threave Estate north of the Solway. To spot one in eastern Scotland would be a red letter day; a chance not to be missed.

Had I possessed a modicum of common sense, the tactic would have been simply to tour around the countryside, searching out the fields where the pinks were feeding. In those surroundings two bean geese would have stood out merely by virtue of their larger size and I could have watched them at leisure. The follies of youth are such, however, that I decided to stalk the birds on the saltings before they left their roost and so, with two hours to elapse before sunrise, an intrepid birdwatcher was crawling over the marsh grass towards the mud at the tide's edge.

Drawn ever onwards by the murmuring of the pinkfeet, I slithered and scrambled as the grey eastern light gradually strengthened, fervently hoping that I could get close enough to view the birds before they grew restless and departed the estuary in search of their scarce winter victuals. It seemed that I had stumbled for miles over the flat marsh. Wherever a gully gave a little cover I could make good progress but then, as the gutter changed direction and threatened to lead me away from the goose talk, it was necessary to move cautiously and slowly on my belly to reach the sanctuary of another creek. Eventually, just as the sun was poking its head over the far horizon, I arrived at the very edge of the saltings and, to my delight, discovered that the geese were but a hundred yards from my position.

It was a wonderful sight. In the clear light of dawn they stood, preening and ruffling, the refection of each bird perfectly mirrored on the silver surface of the glistening wet mud. Conscious that they might flight off the shore at any minute, I anxiously fumbled for my binoculars and scanned the flock. Any disappointment which might have been felt at not immediately spotting the bean geese was masked by the wonder of witnessing, at such close range, the morning ablutions of almost a thousand pinks.

All hope of seeing the rare visitors had almost dissipated when a group of about a dozen birds from the far side of the flock took to the air, lazily flew in a low arc over the mud and alighted directly in front of me. I could hardly believe my luck. The nearest goose was clearly bigger than a pinkfoot and, through my glasses, I could readily discern the distinctive orange and black bill of a bean. Traversing the remainder of that group with the binoculars, I found that it contained not two but three of the vagrants.

For perhaps fifteen minutes I lay, enthralled by the picture and the sound of so many geese at close quarters. Several other little parties of pinks left the farthest edge of the flock to resettle beside my precious bean geese and it was then that I realised that they were leapfrogging towards me, pushed closer by the advancing flow of the tide. Then, as if to break the pattern, one group took to the air, circled the birds still on the mud and headed inland. In an instant the great flock fell silent. Three or four seconds elapsed and suddenly, with a tremendous clamour of calling and thrashing wings, the entire company rose into the sky and passed directly over my head.

Rolling over on to my back I watched the birds gain height before sorting themselves out into tidy V-shaped skeins. As they spread out over the marsh, their music subsided to the well known "wink-wink" notes which are so characteristic of the species.

Scrambling to my feet to gain a better view of the departing geese, I heard two gunshots ring out over the saltings and watched a pair of birds fall out of the lowest skein. For some months I had been aware that, on those early morning sorties, I shared the marsh with other human beings who had a purpose other than simply watching the wildfowl. Sometimes I would find their motor cars already parked at the side of the coast road when I arrived but they always seemed to leave for home before I returned to the sea wall. On one occasion I had seen a far figure and his dog half a mile ahead of me but I had never made contact with one of those wildfowlers and harboured a slight regret that they disturbed the lonely tranquillity of the foreshore. That morning, as I stood watching the flighting skeins, I prayed that neither of the birds which had succumbed to the fowler's shots would be the very bean geese which, minutes earlier, had paraded on the mud a stone's throw from me.

Only then did I remember that the tide was fast advancing. Already water was flowing up some of the gutters in the marsh grass and little trips of waders flew back and forth as the sea covered their feeding grounds. Conscious that I had a long way to walk and that the tidal flow would be fairly rapid over the flat marsh, I decided to delay no longer. Not that I was unduly concerned; my outward journey had been in darkness and my route dictated by the need to remain out of sight of the geese I was stalking. In daylight my progress would be considerably faster.

Following the top of the creek along which I had earlier crawled, my emotions were a peculiar combination of elation at the success of the expedition and worry that, so soon after I had observed them, one or two of the bean geese might have fallen to the wildfowler's gun. Before I had travelled 400 yards, however, I was faced by a more pressing problem. The flooded gully which I expected to lead me back to the roadside, joined with another and I discovered that the land upon which I stood had become an island - an island which would very quickly be covered by the sea.

In vain I searched for a place where the creeks might be sufficiently narrow to jump across. Indeed, they seemed to grow both wider and deeper by the minute. Eventually, reconciled to the clear fact that a soaking could not be avoided, I removed my boots, rolled up my trouser legs and gingerly stepped into the icy water. Once committed, there was no going back but, whereas I had hoped to be able to wade across the gully, it became necessary to swim the final yard. Fortunately, although the air temperature was close to freezing point, there was little wind that morning and, having clambered up the muddy side of the creek, I was able to avoid chilling by running the remaining distance towards high water mark.

That was when I met George Wilson. He must have watched with some incredulity as a wet, bedraggled figure trotted over the saltings towards him. Emerging from a clump of straw coloured rushes, he shouted a greeting and, gasping for breath, I slowed my pace and turned to face the old man. Feeling that an explanation of my condition was required, I blurted out some words about watching geese and being cut off by the tide. The little fellow - he could not have been much more than 5 feet tall - smiled wrily and suggested that I go to his cottage to dry out. He then turned back to his hiding place and re-emerged carrying a long brown shotgun and two dead pinkfeet.

The next few hours were to be amongst the most significant in my life. George Wilson lived in an estate cottage just across the road from the shore, a cottage of which he had been given a life rent in recognition of many years spent as a gamekeeper to the local laird. Sitting by his roaring fire, wrapped in a thick woollen blanket, I listened to his accounts of days and nights spent close to nature. He told me about many stormy mornings in pursuit of the wild geese and about hard times when hunger could be kept at bay only by the wildfowl culled from the estuary or rabbits snared in the hedgerows.

As he related his tales I began to appreciate that this gnarled old man understood far more about the habits of wild birds and animals than any of the guest speakers to whom I had paid avid attention at meetings of the Natural History Society or the Ornithologists Club. He had lived with the rotating seasons for almost three-quarters of a century and little seemed to have escaped his notice.

I will not say that he was impressed; but he was certainly surprised to learn that a mere birdwatcher had risen long before dawn and crawled to the very edge of the saltings in the hope of spying a relatively rare species of goose. He would have understood my behaviour much more readily had it been motivated by the prospect of stocking the larder. But then, he assured me, no wildfowler would have been so foolish as to get himself cut off by the tide.

As we talked that morning I grew to respect the old fowler and, I suspect, he must have developed a liking for me. Dusty diaries and photographs were produced, he showed me how to clean his ancient hammer gun and took great delight in demonstrating to me the antiquated equipment with which he reloaded his spent cartridge cases. Above all, he talked with real affection and sympathy about the wild birds of the estuary and, without trying, persuaded me that one could never really know about wildlife until one had hunted it on terms which favoured the quarry rather than the hunter. The gesture was at the time wasted upon my youthful arrogance but I later appreciated just what an honour it was when, before I departed from his cottage that day, George Wilson invited me to accompany him on a wildfowling outing the following weekend.

I could hardly wait and, as the days slowly passed, I rehearsed over and over again the instructions which had been given. Saturday arrived at last, bringing with it a hard frost so that the stars twinkled brightly from a cloudless sky as I pedalled my bicycle along the winding coast road, the saddlebag stuffed with all of the clothing which George had specified. Arriving almost an hour ahead of the appointed time and expecting a long cold wait before my mentor rose from the comfort of his own bed, I was surprised to find that a light already glowed in his parlour window and that a hearty fire burned in his grate with a black kettle on the boil to provide steaming mugs of hot, sweet tea.

While he busied himself collecting together gun, cartridges and all of the other accoutrements which apparently were necessary for a visit to the shore, I listened to the plan which he had set for the day. Because the tide would be higher than the previous Saturday, he reckoned that the geese would be roosting a mile to the east and, to intercept them, we would need to follow the river channel and find a place to hide just where the saltmarsh changed to dunes and sandy beach. Then, after the great grey birds had flighted, he would welcome my assistance with some mysterious "wee job" before returning to the marsh for a shot at the duck in the afternoon.

The sky was still inky black as we stepped out into the frosty morning air. From the woods behind George's house an owl hooted and, as if in reply, a far-off engine gave a double toot as it pulled the London sleeper train along the old LNER line towards Edinburgh.

Burdened by the weight of the old man's gun and a hessian sack of other equipment, I was soon out of breath trying to keep up with the tiny figure which strode purposefully along the metalled road. Apart from a milk lorry, its load of bottles rattling menacingly in their metal crates as it thundered past, we saw no sign of life until we reached the village where, to my relief, George paused for a moment to buy half a dozen breakfast rolls at the bakery. The warm, yeasty aroma from the bakehouse served to recharge my batteries; which was just as well for, a few paces farther down the street my companion - a gentlemen to the last - ordered me to lay down the gun and carry two weighty bundles of newspapers, which lay on the pavement, into the village store.

"Mrs Simpson has a bad back," he explained. The fact hardly surprised me if she had spent a lifetime lugging great bales of newsprint about. Every household in the surrounding area must have read at least three morning papers to justify the pile which that little shop purveyed.

There was the merest tinge of grey spreading upwards in the eastern sky as we left behind the streets and crossed a long rickety wooden bridge which traversed the rivermouth. Climbing down the grassy banking to the flats below, George warned me against allowing any mud to enter the barrels of his precious fowling piece. Such mischance, he warranted, would result in his head being blown off should he fire the weapon while its muzzles were blocked. It seemed to me that he could always look down the tubes before loading any cartridges but, that morning, I was not inclined to argue with my tutor and guide.

Feeling like a beast of burden I trudged onwards in the wake of the wiry wee fellow until the mud changed to soft yellow sand and I realised that we were on a beach which was familiar from boyhood bathing parties and family picnics. As the silhouettes of the ramshackle wooden changing huts came into view, George suddenly made a left turn across the high water mark and kept up his forced march for another few hundred yards. Without warning he stopped, so that I almost blundered into him, and declared that this was the place.

"The pinks are out there," he avowed although, strain my ears as I might, I could not hear any of the notes which his keen senses had discerned.

"Tip out that big bag," he instructed. Grateful that the dead weight of the sack could at last be removed from my shoulders, I hastily obliged and spread out on the damp sand three smaller bags, a rusty biscuit tin and something which, at first, I thought to be a tent. In fact, I was not far from the mark. George took the bundle of canvas and opened it out on the ground, explaining that it was the mainsheet from an army ridge tent which, while serving His Majesty, he had identified as being ideal for a morning just such as this.

Lying on our backs, with the sand-coloured fabric doubled over our bodies, we must have been as near to invisible as it is possible to be on a featureless shore. While we waited, the old fellow explained the procedure to be followed. With our heads resting on two of the smaller bags which had been contained in the heavy sack and the canvas drawn up to our noses, we would lie absolutely still until the geese were directly overhead. Then, when he gave the word, I was to throw back the sheeting so that he could spring to his feet and fire both barrels. While he reloaded the weapon, I would sprint out to collect the two fallen geese and, without any delay, return to lie flat in the tent-cloth to await the next skein.

It did not quite work out like that. We lay for the better part of an hour with the cold gradually seeping up from the damp ground before there was any movement from the pinkfeet. When they did flight, the birds came, not in a timed succession of small groups, but as one huge flock which filled the dawn sky. Filled the sky, that is, apart from the section immediately above our encampment.

Afraid to move lest I incurred the wrath of my tent-mate, I attempted to roll my eyes to impossible angles so that I might watch the departing geese. The still air was saturated by their music but the nearest birds flew past at least a hundred yards to our side.

Although I had never heard George swear, I fully expected to be treated to a rich vocabulary of curses on account of our bad luck. On the contrary, after the last of the goose-talk had subsided, he merely raised himself on one elbow and said "That was close, laddie, verrae close."

The "wee job" which George had lined up for me turned out to be quite a treat. One of his cronies, Bert Nicholson, had been hospitalised due to a tractor accident and his collection of penned wildfowl required to be fed and watered. Bert's house was on the same estate as George's, the two men having been workmates for most of their lives. Behind the house, where most folk might have a vegetable garden, three shallow ponds had been excavated and a strong perimeter fence of wire netting provided sanctuary for an odd miscellany of duck and geese.

The collection had apparently been started with wingtipped birds which local wildfowlers brought to Bert but, as his interest in the subject had expanded, the farmhand bought in breeding pairs of duck to augment his stock. Inside the netting were almost a hundred birds representing most of the native species plus a staggering variety of fancy foreign duck. My interest, however, was on the field behind the pens where a small flock of greylag geese grazed, accompanied by little parties of free-flying mallard, pintail and wigeon. Those birds, George assured me, were not part of the collection but had voluntarily accepted the free rations which Bert supplied and remained unmolested in the field for most of the winter. As if to prove the point, 20 or 30 greylag took to the air as he spoke and noisily circled around the house before alighting to resume their feeding on a fresh portion of the pasture.

After tending to the penned wildfowl, we sat by the side of the ponds and ate our own lunch. During this time I was given a goodly dose of homespun philosophy relating to the sport of wildfowling and, before long, I began to appreciate why a man who, on the face of it, had risen long before dawn on a freezing December morning for the apparent purpose of shooting geese, was not noticeably disappointed when the great battalions of birds flew past just out of range. I learned about the challenge of the pursuit and about the thrill of seeing and hearing wild fowl in wild places. Above all, I learned that an old man who had suffered the shelling of the Great War, whose wife and small child had been killed by lightning while he was overseas in the army and who had survived the depression of the 1930s, could find peace and contentment when sharing the dark estuary with the birds which he loved.

After listening to George's story I felt like an intruder when we went back to the shore for the evening flight. As darkness fell and wigeon whistled overhead I thought of all that he had told me and wished that I could creep away and leave him to enjoy the solitude he relished so much. In the event, I twice had to run out and fetch the duck which fell to the boom of his 8-bore so perhaps, by combining the duties of gun-bearer and retriever, I earned my place by his side that day.

What I certainly did not earn was the present which he gave me two weeks later. Having persuaded my parents that George should be invited to share our Christmas dinner, the old fowler arrived at our house in a taxi, dressed in his Sunday suit and bearing a long, thin parcel neatly wrapped in brown paper. He explained that he would never again use the gun which he had carried for so many years on his gamekeeper's rounds and he would like to think that, unlike himself, it could avoid permanent retirement. It was a Birmingham 12-bore bearing the name of a North Berwick ironmonger and, in every sense, it had been built as a keeper's tool rather than a work of art. Despite its plain stock and unengraved action, I was to treasure that gun for a

long time. I also grew to treasure the fact that it changed me from a birdwatcher into a wildfowler.

Chapter 2

Exploring New Foreshores

Indentured to George Wilson, my fowling apprenticeship was spent on the expansive, windswept foreshores of East Lothian. Together we shared many golden dawns and dusks, together we battled against gale-driven sleet, together we prepared for the start of each new season.

Time passed and many things changed. First my studies and later a wife demanded an increasing share of my scarce leisure hours. The marshes upon which George and I met became a nature reserve and a permit scheme was introduced to control wildfowling. Finally, in his 80th year, George passed on to those great saltings in the sky.

Other, more subtle, changes were also taking place. Politicians told the nation that "we had never had it so good" and one effect of the new prosperity was a huge increase in motor car ownership. In consequence, those coastal areas where wildfowl congregated in winter became accessible to greater numbers of visiting fowlers. Within the population at large, increased opportunities for access to the countryside brought a heightened awareness of the problems facing wildlife. In the minds of many townspeople the threats to wild birds and animals included not only pollution, industrialisation, pesticides and intensive agriculture but also traditional country sports. Along with his colleagues in other branches of fieldsports, the wildfowler was faced with the urgent need to demonstrate that his activities were conducted responsibly with due attention to practical conservation.

In response to those changes, wildfowling clubs began to be formed throughout the land. It was hardly surprising that many of the old breed of fowler resented this development challenging, as it did, the uniquely individual nature of his sport. What did not change, however, was the ancient relationship between each wildfowler and his quarry in that dark hour before dawn in the solitude of a remote marsh. As the world around grew faster, as the pressure of everyday life became ever more intense, so too did many wildfowlers grow to value even more highly the respite afforded by hours spent with dog and gun on the lonely saltings.

One of the problems facing any wildfowler who also has to earn his daily bread is the possibility that his work will take him far away from the coast. In this case, "far" means any distance greater than an hour's car journey from the estuarine flightlines. The corollary of this is that, in seeking new employment, he will most closely scan the "Situations Vacant" columns for jobs in prime fowling country. It was not, therefore, solely good chance which found me uprooting family, goods and chattels to move to a situation where both my home and my office were situated within a twenty minute drive of three major estuaries.

Although I had harboured my own doubts about the desirability of organising fowlers into clubs and associations, it proved to be a considerable advantage to be able to join just such a body when faced with the need to explore a new area. There can be few other methods of making all the necessary contacts so effectively or so quickly.

The club which accepted my membership application had been in existence for only a couple of years and had been formed specifically for the purpose of persuading the County Council to declare a Local Nature Reserve on an estuary. For some time the quality of sport on the foreshore had been steadily declining and, rather than helplessly watch their wildfowling heritage disappear, those local worthies took the brave decision to seek some forms of control before it was too late.

Their battle with bureaucracy was to prove difficult and protracted. From the early enthusiasm which abounded when I joined that club, there were passages during which gloom and despondency reigned and times when we were all tempted to give up the fight. Finally, 17 years after the first application to the Council officials had been lodged, the necessary declaration was enacted and bye-laws were introduced.

The preoccupation with forming a nature reserve did not stand in the way of many other club activities and, during those early years, I was able to make new friends and become familiar with stretches of coastline which, for almost two decades, would provide the mainstay of my sport. Incidental to the main wildfowling focus of the club, but important from the point of view of maintaining a corporate identity, were the annual clay pigeon shoot and gundog tests. The former eventually persuaded me to lay aside George Wilson's old side-by-side shotgun and experiment with the over-and-under design which was slowly gaining popularity while the gundog tests gave an incentive to improve upon my earliest attempts at dog training.

During the autumn and winter, however, it was the wild estuaries which commanded both time and attention and one fellow member of the club played a greater part than most in those early exploits. Andrew had not benefited from the type of apprenticeship which I had served in the Lothians but he did come to wildfowling with considerable experience of roughshooting. Such is the addictive nature of fowling that, before long, he virtually forsook his days shooting woodpigeons or rabbits in order to devote his weekends to the more fulfilling pursuit of duck and geese.

During much of our first season together we retricted our activities to a few well-used sections of the shore and, in consequence, suffered from a common problem of the times. Although we might rise very early in the morning and travel to the estuaries long before first light, it was a race to secure the best positions before any other gunners arrived. Despite this, we did succeed in finding reasonable sport and, more crucially, became thoroughly familiar with much of the ground and the local habits of the fowl.

Towards the end of that winter we began to range farther afield and, as a result, met up with two visiting fowlers who always had a lively tale to relate. Yapper Mike and Oil Can John hailed from near Hull where, we were assured, such nicknames are neither derogatory nor uncommon amongst the fisher folk. Several years later one of my own less auspicious wildfowling outings corresponded with one of the Hull lads' most memorable.

I suppose that fishing for Icelandic cod must harden any man to the foulest of weather and nothing which a Scottish winter could throw at those two stalwarts would deter them from braving the shore of the Firth. On the morning in question, the BBC shipping forecast had promised "Sea areas Cromarty, Forth and Tyne - gale force 8, increasing severe gale 9, north veering north easterly, imminent." Mike and John could hardly sleep - not because their caravan was being buffeted by the rising wind but due to excitement at the prospect of a worthwhile flight. An earlier sortie in January had drawn blank and this would be their last chance to shoot a goose before another season drew to a close.

Their own description of the weather that day suggested that the Met. Office had seriously underestimated the wind force and the fact that it carried sleet in its teeth merely added to the attraction. Arriving at the normally crowded car parking area to find it totally deserted, the two trawlermen were able to pick a prime position before settling down with their backs to the gale to await the action.

They did not have long to reflect upon the prospects. Before the first streaks of daylight appeared through the racing clouds, great packs of wigeon began pouring over their gully seeking the doubtful sanctuary of the sandbanks in the middle of the estuary. With a near-hurricane in their tails, the duck presented well-nigh impossible shots as they were whipped overhead and a whole box of cartridges had been fired before Mike and John realised that, in the unlikely event of connecting with a bird, it would be swept out to sea before it could be picked.

The geese were a different matter altogether. Dawn was well advanced before the greylags decided that hunger could be ignored no longer and, for more than an hour, ragged skeins battled against the weather to reach the fields beyond the sea wall. It takes considerable determination to keep the gun barrels swinging at geese which seem to present an almost stationary target but the two lads quickly got the hang of the technique and ended the flight with three birds apiece. Had they not showed admirable restraint, there is no doubt that they could have executed considerable slaughter but, being true wildfowlers, they knew when to stop.

Now it so happened that on that very February morning I was ensconced on the south shore of that selfsame estuary, driving conditions having been so perilous that there was not time to motor round to the other side. If ever there was a case of contrasting fortunes, that was it. While Yapper and Oil Can were enjoying the flight of their lives, it was a miserable wildfowler who ended the morning frozen, soaking and half blind. Of duck I saw not a sign but this did not in any way dampen my enthusiasm as it seemed certain that the howling wind would keep any geese which braved the elements close enough to the ground to offer a sporting shot. Finding cover on the marsh was difficult as the gale was flattening the sparse reed fringes. Hopefully, however, the birds would be too preoccupied with the flying conditions to pay too much attention to hazards below.

Perversely, as Mike and John were already discovering to their delight, the greylags had opted to flight against the wind and very few came to the south side. Those which did passed half a mile along the sea wall, clearly bound for some prime feeding about which they had knowledge but of which I was ignorant. Normally it is worth remaining on the saltings until one is certain that all the geese have left the roost but so miserable had I become, as a result of sleet stinging against my face and being blown down my neck, that after a couple of hours of self-imposed torture, I elected to call it a day.

Then the inevitable happened. The gun had no sooner been securely fastened into its slip than four greys sped straight for me. Fumbling with frozen hands, my weapon was pulled out again and a single cartridge thrust into one chamber as the hindmost bird passed overhead. I threw up the gun and, just as the barrels caught up with the tail of the goose, a contact lens was whipped out of my right eye by the wind.

A very strange phenomenon occurs to we shortsighted individuals under such circumstances. Deprived of clear vision in the master eye, the left eye took over and an unconscious "correction" of swing was applied. There was nothing I could do to prevent the shot charge from passing harmlessly a yard to the right of the greylag's starboard wing.

Trying to find a ¬-inch disc of clear perspex on a storm-lashed shore is a futile task and my mood did not even permit an attempt. Fortunately a pair of spectacles was kept on the parcel shelf of the Land-Rover so I was not stranded due to lack of vision. Nevertheless, it was a somewhat dejected fowler who headed down the road. To complete an utterly miserable morning, the sleet turned to snow and formed massive drifts along the foothills. My slight smugness that 4-wheel drive would cope with the conditions was soon dispersed when I discovered that several vehicles had been caught out by the sudden worsening of the weather and the way ahead was well and truly blocked. Just to add a final touch, by the time that I had turned the Land-Rover, an articulated lorry had become trapped behind me and all escapes were thwarted.

Being stuck in a snowdrift is bad enough at the best of times but when you are soaked to the skin, cold, hungry and convinced that a dose of flu is on its way, the ordeal must be experienced to be believed. It was almost dark before the snow ploughs had cleared the road and a worried spouse failed to give the sympathy which was so richly deserved. The subsequent telephone call from Mike and John simply rubbed salt into my wounds and I later had to explain to them the reason for my lack of enthusiasm for their success that day.

The experience of losing a contact lens not only weakened my faith in such fragile articles, it also brought home just how much wildfowlers rely upon their senses. But, if eyesight is absolutely essential to the participant in any shooting sport, the longshore gunner also depends heavily upon his other faculties if he is to fully appreciate the wonder of the environment within which he pursues his quarry.

The haunting call of grey geese as they grow restless on their roost far out on the saltings, the piping whistle of a cock wigeon flighting over the sea wall at dusk, the unremitting howl of a January gale which drives stinging rain across the pre-dawn marsh or the persistent rustle from the reed verges of an estuary as a labrador struggles to carry a heavy mallard drake through the thick, dense stalks. All these are familiar sounds to the wildfowler, notes which feature prominently in the symphonic poetry of his sport.

A keen sense of hearing is of immense benefit to the coastal gunner, not only so that he may fully appreciate the natural chorus which pervades his hunting ground but also that he might receive a timely warning of approaching duck or geese. There are those who scoff at the notion of wearing hearing protection while shooting but they unquestionably run a serious risk of suffering impairment of that vital faculty in the middle years of their lives. I must confess to once being doubting of the good advice I was offered in this regard but, before I had been shooting for many years, I had encountered so many half-deaf fowlers that I rapidly revised my opinion. Fortunately it is possible to obtain unobtrusive little earplugs which keep out the damaging high frequencies of a gun blast without interfering with normal hearing.

Never is aural perception more important than when wildfowling by moonlight. There is something rather special about flighting geese or duck under a silvery moon and it is an aspect of the sport which will unfailingly provide a rich collection of memories, many of which will be focused around the profusion of sounds to which the night-time fowler is exposed.

For a few nights either side of the full moon, given favourable weather conditions, wildfowl will flight to and from their feeding grounds much as they do at dawn or dusk. In mid-winter the hours of daylight are short and gone is the abundance of waste grain, potatoes and fresh grass which lay in the autumn fields. As a result, hungry birds willingly take the opportunity of bright moonlight to search for extra victuals. This night traffic normally commences an hour or two after the moon has risen and it may continue almost until dawn approaches. Indeed, many wildfowlers have discovered that morning flight frequently is less intense at times of the full moon on account of those nocturnal activities of the fowl.

Although there are six full cycles of the moon during each fowling season, not all provide suitable conditions for shooting. Cloud cover is of paramount importance; too much or too little and the task becomes virtually impossible. Ideally we want a thin veil of cloud to provide a light background against which the birds will appear in silhouette as they approach. A clear night sky is inky black and almost nothing will be seen and, believe me, frustration runs high when the sound of geese or duck alerts the fowler's trigger finger but his quarry passes over invisible beneath the twinkling stars. Perhaps it is because night shooting is such an infrequent pleasure that each occasion is particularly memorable.

During the year following the episode with the lost contact lens, the weather gods were especially unkind and the October, November and December moons were each obliterated by dark, heavy clouds. Knowing that January might provide the last chance, the radio was anxiously tuned to the meteorological forecasts as the month progressed. Snow had lain in the fields for almost a week and the approach of the full moon was heralded by several nights of cloudless skies and hard frosts. Not having managed a moonflight at all that season, there was despair in my breast that the final opportunity might pass without a wisp of cloud to lighten the sky.

On the 24th of the month I decided that I could wait no longer so, as soon as parental duties had been completed by the ritual reading of bedtime stories, I packed the car with dog, gun, waders and a camouflage net and set a course to the estuary. Travelling north it was noticeable that the snow cover became thicker with each mile and doubt crept into my mind as to whether the geese would be finding much to eat in the fields. A slight change of plan seemed appropriate to accommodate the distinct possibility that normal wildfowl behaviour patterns might be upset by this factor so, instead of turning down to the mudflats, I kept driving until the foreshore changed from glutinous ooze to grassed saltings.

Eventually I found a likely spot and steered down a rutted farm track where, by good fortune, a cowhand was still at work in a brightly lit byre. After establishing that there would be no objection to a wildfowler parking on the land, the car was unpacked and I followed Meg as she used her canine instinct to choose the safest path down to the shore. Where the snow-covered marsh had been washed by the tide there were little islands of green vegetation amid the frozen merse and it was to the most extensive of those that we headed, calculating that if the geese were to move at all that night, it would be to such an area.

The striking of a distant village clock and the crunch of my boots on the frozen marsh grass were the only sounds to be heard as I warily picked my way over the foreshore to the chosen place but then, as the hide was set up and I settled down in a shallow gutter, new noises became apparent. Far out on the merse the tide turned, causing flocks of wading birds to pipe their shrill complaint as they were slowly moved forward by the incoming waves. From time to time an eerie crackling was produced by the flow of the sea under packed ice in each frozen gully and creek. Then, my senses alerted by Meg's tail suddenly beginning to wag, I strained my ears to discern the music of flighting pinkfeet a mile or so down river.

Before long I noticed that a thin layer of cloud was slowly spreading from the east, producing the effect of a delicate net curtain being drawn across the night sky. For the first time that season it began to look as though the weather conditions might be perfect for a moonflight and, if I finally returned home with an empty bag, I should have to look to my own shortcomings to provide an excuse.

I very rarely use decoys below the sea wall and, on that evening, I had not thought to take any surrogate duck or geese. Surveying the panorama before me and knowing that any sign of feeding birds would bring others tumbling in, I rather regretted not having prepared better for the campaign. No sooner had that thought passed through my mind than several dozen plover wheeled out of the heavens and settled thirty yards from my position. Time passed and by midnight I was beginning to feel the chill night air creeping through my thermal underwear. Although I had heard some geese flighting to the east, no more fowl had come to investigate my green oasis. Then it happened.

A double whistle broke the silence and, as the Beretta was raised in anticipation, a pair of wigeon circled into range. Two shots, two thumps and the air was full of plover noisily protesting at the interruption to their feast. By the time that Meg had retrieved both duck, the flock of waders had settled once more and were feeding as if nothing had occurred. For the next hour wildfowl virtually queued up to come into that little patch of green set in a white wilderness. Presumably hunger pangs had finally persuaded them to seek out a likely source of food and, when I ran out of cartridges at 1.30 am, two more wigeon, one mallard, two pinkfeet and a greylag had been added to the bag. Eight birds for ten shots - not a greedy cull by any standards but a better tally than normally can be expected on the foreshore.

Why is it that if someone invites me to shoot pheasants or a farmer calls to complain that he is plagued by woodpigeon, I never take less than twice as many cartridges as I expect to use but, when wildfowling, I rarely pocket more than a handful of shells? Perhaps it is to sustain dreams. Had an extra box been available that night I might have doubled the bag. On the other hand it is highly probable that the flight would have petered out a few minutes later and I would have sat freezing on the saltings until daybreak with the magic of the night slowly dissipating as numb fingers or a damp backside cried for relief.

Next day I was telling Andrew about my adventure under the moon and he confessed that it was an angle of the sport which he had never tried although, as an accomplished naturalist, he well knew the flighting habits of the fowl. I explained to him that conservation-minded fowlers particularly welcome the opportunity to go night-flighting on account of the fact that disturbance to the marsh by gunshot is much lessened during the hours of darkness. Also, because shots are generally taken at closer range, there is less chance of merely wounding a bird than at dawn or dusk. As I finished the story, the look in his eyes allowed me to anticipate his request and we quickly arranged a rendezvous for the coming evening.

As the moon was scheduled to rise more than an hour later than on the previous night, it was agreed that instead of returning to the estuary, we should attempt to intercept the pinkfooted geese which roosted on the Big Loch. If the fowl were co-operative, this plan would allow us to enjoy a couple of hours at the water's edge and still get home at a respectable time. In effect, it would be very similar to a morning flight except that the moon, rather than the rising sun, would occupy the eastern sky.

At the appointed hour I found Andrew already waiting at the old farm gate, his bright-eyed yellow labrador wearing the camouflaged doggy-jacket for which it was famed in the locality. Although half a mile separated us from the loch, the strains of goose music carried clearly through the still night air, prompting two impatient fowlers to waste no time in donning waterproofs and boots.

The short walk through the moonlit fields was in itself full of interest and, had we been in less of a hurry, we might have tarried to watch the antics of a large, red dog fox hunting in the verges. A flock of blackfaced sheep, taking advantage of the full moon to graze the sparse winter grass, demonstrated no sign of alarm at the presence of their vulpine companion and I wondered whether they would have been so unperturbed had they young lambs at heel. As we approached the narrow band of stunted alders which divide the arable land from the lochside reedbeds we did pause for a few seconds to admire the silent flight of an owl searching for its supper amongst the frost-flattened rushes. Twice it stooped, a ghostly form in the moonlight, and on the second attempt was rewarded with a mouse or some other small mammal.

When we moved on, Andrew whispered that the sound of the geese and the sight of fox and owl had already made his outing worthwhile; a comment which heartened me somewhat as it had become clear, during our walk from the cars, that most of the pinkfeet were roosting off the Policies Shore - a section of the loch which was outwith our boundaries.

At the lochside we found adequate cover without resorting to erecting hides so, spaced forty yards apart, we settled down to wait for the pinks to move. Above our heads the naked branches of the trees stood out in sharp profile against the thin clouds and my sole regret was that only the merest hint of a breeze ruffled the expansive surface of the water. It is rare to find the ideal combination of a brightly illuminated sky and galeforce winds but I rather wished that Andrew could have experienced such perfection on his first attempt at a moonflight. On the other hand, my optimism was boosted a little when a small group of thirty or forty geese lifted from the water half a mile to the west and settled again within fifty yards of our position.

During the next half hour there occurred several similar movements of birds until well over two hundred pinkfeet were swimming close to our shoreline. I knew that Andrew's pulse would have quickened to keep pace with my own and I suspected that his dog, like Meg, would be restlessly quivering in anticipation. Then, with a tumultuous clamour, a huge flock of geese took off from the Policies Shore area and circled close to the water before sorting itself out into three orderly skeins. Those birds passed inland well out of gunshot range but their noisy departure caused the pinkfeet in front of us to grow restless and I knew that it would be only a matter of minutes before they too decided to take to the air.

When they did, they performed in textbook style. Their low murmuring grew slightly in intensity before abruptly ceasing altogether. There was complete silence for about two seconds and then, with the characteristic babble of geese lifting from their roost, the flock took off directly into the gentle wind, gained a little height and turned towards the shore. Unfortunately, although the pinks had acted according to the book, I had failed to take account of the basic rules by remaining in position after the geese first settled on the water in front. Had I interpreted the signs correctly, I should have moved sixty or seventy yards west so as to have been underneath their flightpath. As it was, I could only watch impotently as they passed over to my right.

Andrew, on the other hand, found himself just within range and I saw his gun barrels swing upwards before a single shot brought the nearest goose tumbling out of the sky. That bird safely retrieved we stood for a few minutes, marvelling at the silver patterns of moonlight on the waters of the loch, before happily retracing our steps to the farm gate. Of the owl nor the fox we could find no trace but sheep were still grazing contentedly in the fields and sporadic bursts of goose talk told us that plenty of pinkfeet remained on the roost.

One of the talents which George Wilson had possessed but which I never succeeded in mastering was the art of calling geese by mouth. Often I had marvelled as my old mentor persuaded an entire skein of flighting birds to change direction, simply by uttering a few vocal notes.

Shortly after I moved farther north I teamed up with Bill Purves, a veteran of countless seasons and a man who also could call geese from the skies. Unlike George, however, Bill relied upon wooden instruments to produce the requisite music and, from his instructions, I gradually acquired some of that skill.

Not that the employment of goose calls is particularly useful at morning flight. At such times the geese know where they are going and are unlikely to break their journey to investigate a would-be pied piper hidden on the saltings. Despite this fact, one of the antics which never ceases to raise a smile amongst old hands is the inappropriate use of wooden or plastic calls. The devices are widely sold and many newcomers to the sport seem to believe that they have magical properties below the sea wall.

One of Bill Purves' favourite stories related to a morning when he became intrigued by two visitors to the estuary who appeared to be having a two-way conversation on their calls. Situated between the two, Bill decided to join in and dug his own call from deep in his coat pocket. He also had a mouth organ tucked away and this, too, he pulled out. Knowing Bill's prowess with both instruments I have no difficulty in believing that he successfully fooled the novices into thinking that there was a real goose hidden in the reeds. The way he tells the tale, both men left their places and crept towards him, meeting some 20 yards from where he was honking. They then stole forward together and, just as they reached the edge of Bill's gully, he changed from the sound of a distressed greylag to a harmonica rendering of "Scotland the Brave." Judging from the language which the two stooges are reported to have used, they appreciated neither Bill's prank nor his choice of anthem.

When tide-flighting during the middle of the day there are occasions when the use of duck calls can be of assistance. Not long after joining the wildfowling club I was taken by Bill to a part of the estuary which I had not previously visited. Morning flight drew a complete blank but, to couple some further exploration of the area with the chance to collect a duck or two, we remained on the shore after the sun had risen.

At around 10.00 am the tide turned and began to flow over the marsh. It was not a particularly stormy day yet we hoped that the advancing water might cause some wigeon to flight along the tideline as their favourite preening stations became submerged by the sea. Scanning the marsh with binoculars it was disheartening to note that the few duck which were visible had chosen to roost on the waves rather than on the saltings. More in hope than in expectation, we selected a deep, muddy creek which allowed us to stand upright while remaining well hidden.

Two hours elapsed and three times we were forced to move back along our gully by the rising water. Then, quite suddenly, the breeze changed direction, strengthened and dark clouds appeared over the ridge of hills which formed the southern horizon. Within ten minutes rain was being blown into our faces and that seemed to provide the signal for the duck to move. The first little parties passed well out of shotgun range and it appeared that a regular flightline was developing sixty yards from our hiding place.

Rather than attempt to crawl forward to intercept the fowl, Bill suggested that he would call them into range. From his voluminous pockets he produced a carved rosewood mallard quacker and a homemade wigeon whistle consisting of a 12-bore cartridge case and a 20-bore case, each with the primer removed. By sliding one inside the other while he blew through the primer hole, a variety of pitches of note could be produced.

The next bird on the scene was a single mallard drake. Flying low and taking exactly the line of the earlier duck, I was sure that it, too, would pass out of shot. Bill put the wooden call to his lips and, with hands cupped over the instrument, gave one quack followed by a few seconds of low chattering noise. The drake increased the speed of its wing beat, rose several yards higher and then turned to sweep down on our position. Bill's magnum barked once, dropping the bird right into our creek.

Before the flowing tide finally drove us off the shore, four more mallard paid the price for responding to the artificial quacker. During that time a number of wigeon flighted past but they appeared to be oblivious to the whistles which Bill emitted. A large spring of teal similarly failed to respond but, with five fat duck in the bag, we left the marsh knowing that we had five more than would have been possible without the aid of Bill's wooden call.

Chapter 3

Fowl Weather

The man who shoots partridges over an September stubble may delight in the warmth of the early autumn sun on his back as he relaxes whilst awaiting the next drive. When driven pheasants are the order of the day, what better than a crisp frosty morning with the merest whisper of a breeze and a cloudless blue sky? But the wildfowler's most stirring memories will inevitably involve a howling gale, dark storm clouds and, for good measure, torrential rain. When the weather turns to the cruellest extreme that our fickle climate can produce, then the longshore gunner will relish every minute spent below the sea wall.

Despite the international reputation which the British have for complaining about the weather, a real raging tempest is an infrequent occurrence on our coasts. Only once or twice each winter will the optimum combination of conditions coincide and lucky is the man who can pick up his gun and head for the marsh as soon as the isobars on the weather chart threaten to merge into a single thick black line.

Early one season an unexpected storm provided just such an opportunity to make an unscheduled visit to the estuary. Plans of spending a lazy evening immersed in a good novel were rudely interrupted by rising winds and the sudden onset of a bucketing deluge. Soaked to the skin following a quick run around the garden to shut in the chickens and tie down the beehives, there was really no other possible course of action than to look out gun, cartridges, waterproofs and wellingtons in the hope that the foul weather would remain until morning.

Despite many years of wildfowling, I have singularly failed to learn how to fall asleep on nights such as that. I lay fitfully awake, listening to the rain battering against my bedroom window and to the telltale overflow which indicated a roof gutter blocked by autumn leaves. I suppose that I must have dozed intermittently but, long before the alarm clock was due to sound, I was out of bed and preparing an early breakfast.

Driving to the fowling grounds that morning was not without incident. Because the trees still have some foliage to offer wind resistance, storm damage occurs more readily in autumn than in mid-winter. Several times I was forced to turn the car and make a detour where fallen branches blocked the road. There was also deep flooding on some sections of the route and I was glad to have risen earlier than intended as, otherwise, the delays might have resulted in a missed flight.

Eventually, with windscreen wipers fighting a losing battle against the downpour, I turned along the forest road which led to the shore. Driving down the narrow track, trees were swaying drunkenly in the beam of my headlights making me fearful that, at any minute, several hundredweights of prime spruce might come crashing through the roof. With relief I reached the parking place adjacent to the dunes and, rather than risk a thorough soaking, went through the contortions of donning waterproof overtrousers, coat and boots in the confined interior of the vehicle. Then, with my sou'wester tied firmly on to my head, I opened the door to brave the storm.

So fierce was the tempest that I hesitated before letting Meg out of the car. Moy, my younger labrador, was in peak condition following a few arduous days on the grouse moor but the elderly bitch had the benefit of no such fitness training and, as befitted a companion which had given a canine lifetime of valiant service, was no longer expected to perform any task more strenuous than swimming for a duck in a flight pond or picking a woodpigeon from a clearing in the roosting wood. After a moment's thought, I succumbed to the anthropomorphic notion that Meg would remember the thrill of previous storm flights and would pine unhappily if left behind so, with both dogs at heel, I bowed my head against the gale and set out over the dark sand dunes towards the distant foreshore.

Finding a suitable place to occupy while awaiting dawn proved no easy matter. A little stream which normally meandered over the flats to join the main river had been transformed into a raging torrent. Its gully provided no sanctuary whatsoever and crossing the swirling spate proved to be impossible. Giving up any thoughts of progressing farther along the shore, I settled for the simple expedient of sheltering behind one of the massive concrete blocks which remained as a perpetual reminder of the threat of enemy invasion during Hitler's war.

The hope that there might be geese out on the gale-ravaged mudflats was little more than an act of faith. On other, calmer days I had hidden near that spot listening to the pinkfeet preparing for flight and thrilling to the calling of thousands of dunlin and redshank as they moved in front of the tide. As I removed my gun from its sleeve that morning, no sound was discernible above the howling of the wind and the relentless splatter of the rain against my cement shelter. On account of the dark cloud cover the eastern sky was very slow to lighten and it was some time before white-crested waves could be seen pounding the far mudbanks. At this sight, my spirits rose perceptively. Not only should the unremitting gale cause flighting geese to fly low over the marsh, the state of the sea almost certainly meant that any pinks in the vicinity would have spent the night roosting on the saltings rather than afloat on the water.

There is a positive cosiness to be experienced when sheltering from wild weather. As a boy I had been aware of the sensation whenever a sudden shower of rain sent me scurrying for the refuge of the garden shed or, later, while sitting in a tent listening to a storm flapping at the canvas and watching puddles rapidly forming on the ground outside. Enjoying the private sanctuary provided by the lee of that wartime tank trap I reflected upon those earlier feelings until my reverie was rudely interrupted by Meg snapping to attention.

Picking up the direction of her gaze, I was just in time to see a pack of wigeon streaking past with the wind in their tails. Any chance of a shot was gone before I could mount the gun but their fleeting appearance did serve to put an end to my daydreaming and caused me to consider whether any other duck which came within range should be shot. The normal rule on the marsh at dawn is that no shots should be taken at duck if a goose flight is anticipated lest the sound of gunfire sends the larger fowl fleeing in the opposite direction. On a really stormy morning, however, the risk of this is very much lessened and I resolved that no other wigeon should pass unsaluted.

As it happened, the situation did not arise. The cold grey light of morning slowly extended over the cloudy sky and, although a few small parties of duck could be seen following the course of the flooded stream, none came my way.

I had all but given up hope of getting a shot when Meg again detected birds in the air. Alerted by her tail thumping against my leg, I strained my eyes to pierce the torrential rain and cursed the fact that my misted spectacles hindered rather than aided vision. Then there they were. A ragged skein of about a dozen geese less than 30 yards high and side-slipping across the wind. By the time that I had scrambled to my feet they were almost directly in front. The Beretta barked twice, two pinkfeet folded in mid-air and, their forward momentum virtually unchecked, they slanted down to hit the saltgrass fifty yards along the shore.

By the time that the labradors had returned with those birds, the sky was filled with geese. Skein after skein passed along a mile-wide front, the "wink-wink" of those immediately upwind being just audible above the tempestuous ferocity of the storm. It was an awe-inspiring sight and, although no more passed within shotgun range, I was well pleased with the two in hand.

Opportunities such as those have to be grasped eagerly or else the chance is lost. By lunchtime that day the rain had ceased, the gale had blown itself out and, with the sun drying roads and verges, only a few flood flashes in the fields and some broken branches remained as a legacy of the storm. Those and a pair of pinkfeet hanging in the game larder awaiting the attentions of the skinning knife.

Not all foul weather expeditions are as successful. While a good offshore gale is welcomed by the wildfowler, it is never an easy matter to predict the effect which stormy conditions will have upon the normal flightlines of duck and geese. There was an evening when Andrew and I misjudged things terribly - in more ways than one.

The trip had been planned for several weeks, our intention being to try for a dusk duck flight in the middle basin of the estuary. For such an attempt, the tide had to be well out so that the expansive mudflats would be uncovered at sunset. During the day, along with a small group of friends, we had been walking-up some rather scarce and wily pheasants in a forestry plantation but, due to worsening weather conditions, gave up the shoot at mid-day. Throughout the early afternoon Andrew and I sat in a local roadside caf, discussing the prospects for a good evening flight and watching the rising wind gust the last remaining bronze-coloured leaves from the tall swaying sycamores outside. Our optimism growing with the gale, we decided to have one last cup of tea before setting off for the shore.

When we parked beside the paper mill weir, the rain had stopped but low dark storm clouds scudded across the heavens in the teeth of a near-hurricane. It was a long walk round the perimeter of the airfield but, hastened by the wind on our backs, the journey was made without any delays. Then, calculating that the wild conditions would cause the wigeon to flight close to the winding river channel, we struck out over the mud towards the banks of dark seaweed, to the slimy brown fronds which provided the only cover on that desolate landscape.

Spaced 60 yards apart, we waited and waited. As the sky grew ever darker a few redshank flew low up the river, their plaintive piping hardly competing with the howl of the gale. A pair of shelduck passed with steady, goose-like flight, the bright contrast of their black, white and chestnut plumage seeming starkly out of place amid the all-pervading drabness of the estuary. But, as the dying light of day was finally extinguished, we caught neither sight nor sound of a single wigeon.

In total blackness, Andrew carefully picked his way toward me and we concluded that, in such atrocious weather, the duck must have left the foreshore earlier than usual to seek some sanctuary on inland ponds and flooded fields. Standing, cold and miserable, on those remote mudflats we regretted the hours spent drinking tea in the cafe.

We should then have retraced our steps to the high water mark and followed the grassy banking back to civilisation. So wretched was our condition, though, that we set our aim at the distant lights of the paper mill and attempted to take a shortcut over the mud alongside the foaming river. That was a great mistake. Less than quarter of a mile had been covered before we found ourselves plowtering through soft ooze and, almost simultaneously, we both stuck fast in the glutinous mud.

Luckily, I was able to fall on to my back and remove my feet from the grip of my wellingtons. Andrew, on the other hand, was less fortunate. He lost his balance, tumbled forward and discovered that he could not haul himself out of the thigh waders which he wore. To help him, I had to roll sideways over the thick, wet mud and pull him on to his back. By the time that we had retrieved our footwear and regained firmer ground we were sweating profusely and covered from head to toe in evil-smelling sludge. Two filthy fowlers and two equally filthy dogs drove home in exhausted silence to a somewhat less than rapturous welcome from Andrew's wife. We had used her much-loved little car for the trip and the state of its interior defied description.

The outing which will always rank in my memory as the best ever wildfowling expedition occurred many years ago in weather conditions which would have had most sane people scurrying for the comfort of a warm fireside. For a long time I deliberately avoided retelling this tale because, although there was no great danger to either of the participants, it did not seem wise to encourage any newcomer to the sport to spend a protracted period on a wild shore in mid-winter. I have also always hesitated to make any public mention of double-figure bags of geese because, under normal conditions, responsible wildfowlers will stop shooting after killing two or three of the great grey birds.

The passage of time, the redistribution of wildfowl populations and the increased shooting pressure on the estuary in question now make it unlikely that the feat could be repeated. I am also satisfied that most novices are today sufficiently safety conscious to recognise real danger if they encounter adverse conditions on the marsh. Despite those observations, I will make no excuse for returning later to the questions of safety and excessive bags of fowl.

Peter joined the wildfowling club a few years after me, coming to the area from the Midlands and bringing with him one of the best fowling dogs I have ever known. Zulu was a big, sturdy black labrador with a broad, noble head from which glistened two of the wisest eyes I have ever seen on a dog. Our "flight of a lifetime" was also Zulu's finest hour, a morning when the skill and endurance of man and beast were tested to the limit.

Although we lived in the centre of the Kingdom of Fife and, at any time between October and April, had up to 20,000 geese resident within a 20 mile radius of our homes, Peter and I regularly travelled hundreds of miles in search of new pastures, confident in the belief that, one of those days, we would find a fowlers' Mecca, a marsh which would put our local grounds to shame. With Meg and Zulu in the rear of the Land-Rover we journeyed to Montrose Basin, the Ythan, the wild Firths north of Inverness and, on occasions, deep into the lands south of Hadrian's Wall. We enjoyed some wonderful times, met many wildfowlers throughout the country and, let it be said, had our share of disappointments. Quickly we learned to appreciate that, no matter how highly we had heard a particular estuary or marsh praised, without both skill and local knowledge the visiting fowler was on a hiding to nothing. Peter once calculated that we drove over 300 miles for every bird shot. Certainly, just as at home, we had more blank flights than fruitful ones.

For one particular expedition we had not only loaded the vehicle with all the usual fowling gear but had added sleeping bags and sufficient provisions for an overnight stop. The north shore of the Solway Firth was not exactly uncharted territory as far as we were concerned but we did want to get to know the area better and a two day trip would permit us to explore more of the marsh.

Eastern Scotland had, for over a week, been in the icy grip of a severe freeze-up but, approaching Galloway, we were unprepared for the thick snow cover which lay in the fields and blocked all but the major roads. Even where snow ploughs had cleared a single track, the going was difficult and often we drove between high white walls through which only telegraph poles and the highest trees sprouted skywards. By mid-afternoon we had to engage 4-wheel drive to achieve striking distance of the coast and, despite the benefit of full traction, were eventually forced to abandon the vehicle a mile from the shore.

We had timed our visit to coincide with the full moon in the expectation that we might enjoy an evening flight, spend some hours on the moonlit merse and then retire to the comfort of the Land-Rover for a few hours sleep before returning to the marsh to do business with the fowl in the morning. Our plan was then to travel farther along the coast to sample a different location on the following evening. Taking account of the conditions, however, we elected to carry all of our clothing, together with the food and a camping stove, down to the sea wall and cache them within easy reach of the saltings. That way we would suffer from neither exposure nor hunger if, as appeared likely, the conditions worsened.

A high spring tide covered much of the marsh when we eventually slid our guns from their covers. Watching the light slowly fade from a cold cloudless sky we tried to pick a place where duck might form a flightline but, in the event, darkness fell without a shot being fired. We did hear the music of flighting pinkfeet from farther along the shore but, even had we chosen the right location, they almost certainly would have passed over well out of shot.

There was time for a welcome fry-up before the tide turned and we spent an hour wondering whether another fall of snow might maroon us on the foreshore for a week or more. With only sufficient food for a couple of days, the prospect was not particularly inviting, especially if we were unable to shoot enough fowl to augment our rations. Such idle speculation was, of course, the sort of romantic nonsense to which wildfowlers are prone as, no matter how deep the drifts on the roads, we could readily have walked ten miles along the high water mark to reach a coastal village.

When the moon came up and the water began to recede, we worked our way out over the shore, carefully noting every gutter and taking frequent compass readings as we progressed. With the silver orb of the moon rising higher in the sky a few wigeon began to whistle as they passed overhead but there was no chance to pick out the birds against the inky blackness of the clear sky. For a couple of hours we waited before Peter remarked that the chill had gone out of the air. A westerly breeze began to blow and soon some clouds drifted over, perfectly veiling the heavens and providing exactly the brightly illuminated backdrop for which wildfowlers pray.

For some time we shot steadily as small packs of duck traversed the saltings. A few pinks could be heard in the distance but none came our way. Then, with ominous suddenness, I was aware of a warm blast from the south as the wind abruptly changed direction and, almost immediately, the merse began to to crackle as ice in the creeks and gullies started to thaw. The thin covering of cloud was rapidly dispersed and replaced by dark towering masses which totally obscured the moon and, by the time we had regained the sanctuary of the sea wall with half a dozen wigeon apiece, a strong gale was driving rain across the marsh.

Attempting to steal a few hours sleep in those conditions was futile but, rather than try to return to the Land-Rover, we chose to shelter through the night in the lee of a large hawthorn thicket. In the knowledge that the tide would be flowing again by dawn we checked our bearings and, 90 minutes before the time scheduled for sunrise, headed for a raised portion of the saltings alongside a deep creek. With the storm becoming fiercer by the hour, two tired fowlers positioned themselves 100 yards apart to await the coming of first light.

Handicapped by my spectacles, I was cowering behind a bank, attempting to keep the rain off my face, when the sound of a shot echoed above the unrelenting howl of the wind. Glancing up, I was just in time to see a skein of geese racing towards me, not more than 25 yards above the flattened saltgrass. With the wind in their tails I doubt if their speed was much less than 70 mph and, just as so often happens, it was two hastily taken snap shots which brought a right and left crashing to the ground. Meg ran out, unbidden, to pick up the pinkfeet and she had barely returned with the second bird when another clustered group of seven or eight geese came sweeping over the saltings. This time it was Peter's turn to score a double while I had to be content with a second barrel kill. For half an hour the pinks continued to flight in, providing that superb quality of sport which far surpasses anything offered on the grouse moor or beside a pheasant covert.

Not until I dropped a bird into the gully did I notice the power which was behind the rushing water. Pushed by the incoming tide, the flow should have been upstream but, doubtlessly as a result of the exceptionally heavy rainfall and rapidly melting snow, the brown torrent was gushing out to sea.

Paying absolutely no heed to my shouts, Meg leaped into the raging water to retrieve the goose. Aided by the current she quickly caught up with the dead bird but, when she turned to bring it back, the bitch could make no headway against the stream. Unable to scramble up the steep, slithery sides of the creek, she began to tire and, as the minutes passed, started to slip back in the spate.

Having realised our plight, Peter came over to assist but there was nothing that either of us could do to help the stricken labrador. We watched in helpless horror as the little bitch grew weaker and I was on the edge of panic when Zulu slid down the banking into the gully and swam towards Meg. To our amazement the big dog took the goose from her and, demonstrating enormous power, paddled strongly upstream. Relieved of her burden, Meg succeeded in coming ashore and, although clearly exhausted, ran along the bank keeping pace with Zulu.

Once both dogs were safely on the firm merse we collected up our guns and bags and struggled back in the direction of the sea wall where we laid out nine pinkfeet before brewing a restoring jug of coffee. There were then decisions to be made. The choice lay between trudging back to the Land-Rover, with all our gear and the shot birds, in order that we might attempt to explore a different section of the Firth or, on the other hand, remain where we were for another day and night.

Noting that the thaw was continuing, we opted to stay put. That way, we calculated, there was a good chance that in 24 hours we would be able to drive the vehicle down to the shore and load up at the sea wall.

By mid-day the teeming rain had eased off and, although the gale remained unabated, we were rested and eager to resume our engagement with the fowl. Neither of us had much experience of tide flighting on the Solway but, after scanning the marsh with binoculars, decided that the high wind and fast-flowing tide made the experiment worthwhile. Aware of the dangers presented by such wild conditions on a strange marsh, we were perhaps not as adventurous as the situation demanded and it may be that we missed out on some of the best opportunities. Nevertheless, by continuously falling back before the advancing waves, we did see a lot of duck moving back and forth in their search for sanctuary. Not many passed within gunshot range but, by the time darkness fell, Peter had accounted for several mallard while I succeeded in getting a couple of nice cock teal and a single pintail.

By that time our hawthorn bushes were becoming very familiar and we felt almost at home while, once more, sheltering behind them waiting for the moon to rise. A welcome meal of tinned ham and baked beans was consumed as we laid plans for the night's campaign. We knew that if the events of the previous evening were repeated, we should have the best opportunity of getting under the pinkfeet by moving a mile farther along the saltings. However, faced with the choice of exploring uncharted territory in the dark or settling for the chance of a few wigeon, we opted to merely repeat the sortie of the night before. In view of the success which we had achieved during the morning flight, there was certainly no need to take any risks just for the sake of another few geese.

Rather than separate, Peter and I stayed together in the creek which I had occupied that morning. This strategy enabled both of us to obtain a degree of shelter from the gale, allowed us to watch two directions simultaneously and, most importantly in view of our earlier experience, meant that assistance was readily to hand if any difficulties arose.

The cloud cover was thin and variable with just sufficient moonlight to persuade the fowl to move. At first it looked as though we were to witness a repeat performance of the previous night's sport as small packs of wigeon flighted across the merse. Between us we shot almost a dozen of the whistling duck, with my companion getting the lion's share of the action, before their flightlines altered . As the ebbing tide progressively uncovered more of the saltings, the wigeon chose to frequent the freshly washed saltgrass farther out on the marsh.

For another half hour we sat, enjoying the sensation of being protected from the storm by our deep gutter. Just as we were discussing whether or not it was time to brave the elements and return to the sea wall, the music of pinkfooted geese was carried in on the gale and heavier cartridges were hurriedly loaded in the hope of a shot. The clamour of the geese grew in intensity as the ragged flock approached. Although it is never easy to estimate numbers at night, I guessed that there were over 2000 pinks silhouetted against the moonlit clouds with even more invisible against the darker sky.

For fully five minutes we crouched in that gully watching the geese overhead. There were orderly skeins and disorganised groups, high geese and low, silent parties and noisy. So enthralling was the spectacle that we let them all pass unmolested until the last shootable birds were directly above us. Misjudging their speed, we each had time for only a single shot and, as it happened, mine connected while Peter's went astray. During the wigeon flight I had kept Meg securely tethered by my side so that Zulu had to pick all of our duck but, as the pinkfoot was clearly in sight, lying on firm ground, I decided to release the little bitch to let her regain her confidence after the morning's ordeal. I need not have worried. She bounded out, picked up the dead goose and carried it high as she trotted back to our creek.

Despite our excitement, fatigue was beginning to have its effect and, notwithstanding the mildness of the night, both Peter and I began to feel chilled. It was not quite midnight, the moon was still high in the sky and we could have remained on the marsh in the expectation of getting some sporadic shooting but, surrendering to our shivers and feeling decidedly hungry, we repaired to our base to feed, rest and recover our energies for the morning flight.

It was totally unreasonable to expect another dawn like the one before yet, as the first pale streaks of morning were accompanied by a heightening of the gale and a resumption of the previous day's torrential rain, our anticipation of exciting sport was sharpened.

To add a little variety to the situation, Peter and I swapped places. This unfortunately meant that I had to keep my eyes open, being unable to rely upon the sound of my pal's shots to alert me to approaching birds. Despite my limited vision in those circumstances, the sight which unfolded as daylight strengthened was really quite incredible. Geese passed inland from their roost at the tide's edge, other geese crossed back over the merse after feeding under the moon, duck flew past in all directions and waders circled and spiralled in front of the advancing waves.

The effect of rain on my glasses did nothing to improve my standard of marksmanship but, by the time the marsh had quietened, Meg had retrieved three geese and several duck while Zulu had been working even harder for Peter. Our joint tally for the morning flight amounted to eight pinkfeet, a greylag and a dozen assorted duck.

Buffeted mercilessly by the gale, the trek back to dry land was even more arduous than previously. Eventually, breathless and soaking with sweat, we regained the shelter of the sea wall and thankfully slid down to our beloved hawthorn thicket. After shedding our load and recovering our breath, we drew lots to decide who would walk inland to collect the Land-Rover. Needless to say, I lost and, leaving Peter to guard the guns, dogs and equipment, I trudged up the track to reach the vehicle. For the first time in 36 hours my feet touched a metalled road.

Without any doubt, that was wildfowling with a capital "W". Wild duck and geese in extremely wild conditions provide the ultimate challenge to the sporting Shot. A bag of 19 geese and over 30 duck might seem excessive and certainly there is room to criticise people who kill dozens of geese over decoys or, worse still, shoot them flighting in to a roosting loch at night. Nevertheless, although neither Peter nor I ever shot similar numbers before, or since, we did feel that less than one bird per man-hour in the wildest of winter weather was not an unreasonable reward for enduring such cruel conditions.

To any novice who reads these words, it must be emphasised that although wildfowling in foul weather can be a most exhilarating pursuit, the world of howling winds and racing tides, of oozing mud and treacherous sands, contains many pitfalls for the untutored beginner. The sport of fowling must be learned over many years and any unknown estuary treated with the utmost caution.

Chapter 4

Inland Interludes

Although, almost by definition, wildfowling takes place on the windswept marshes, desolate foreshores and muddy estuaries which extend far below the sea wall, it is possible to shoot duck and geese on inland waterways or, at times, over arable land and rough pasture. In such situations it is vitally important never to take unfair advantage of the fowl but, provided that the unwritten ethics of the sport are observed and any temptation to take large bags is steadfastly resisted, then some exciting adventures may be experienced.

Several years after I joined the local wildfowling club we were, in the middle of a season, offered the shooting rights on Loch Fitty, a 160 acre loch in the south of the county. Arriving to meet the owners one Saturday morning in early November, a sweep of the area with field glasses revealed over 300 mallard and tufted duck riding out a gentle wave. A tour of the perimeter in a motor boat then resulted in dozens of teal springing from the reeds around the edges and it was clear that the marshy ground at either end of the loch also harboured a goodly supply of duck.

The proprietors, whose principal interest in the water was as a put-and-take trout fishery, had erected rough wildfowling hides in strategic positions and advised us that the rental included two boats with outboard engines and the use of the heated fishing lodge for changing before and after flights. The prospect of such unaccustomed luxury, coupled with a glorious abundance of wildfowl, led to the lease being signed without further ado.

At 5.30 am on the following Saturday morning 8 eager club members assembled at the lodge and, as numbers were drawn for hide positions, the discussion centred around such topics as the adequacy of cartridge stocks. Should a bag limit be imposed upon each Gun? If so, should the maximum be set at 8 duck or might 6 birds be more prudent? Would an open-bored skeet gun be more appropriate than a heavy 3" magnum? As it turned out, all of those questions were to remain strictly hypothetical.

Our first indication of impending disaster was presented immediately we trooped out of the lodge. Instead of stepping down from the jetty into the boats, wadered legs had to be swung up over the gunwhales, a week of torrential rain having raised the water level by fully two feet. The second surprise came as we motored out to the hides. Duck which we confidently expected to flight in to the loch at dawn were already there. Many doubtlessly decided that nocturnal boating was not to their liking and forsook the water for more peaceful sanctuaries.

At last, just as the first faint streaks of morning appeared above the eastern horizon, all the Guns were deposited at their allocated positions and our troubles really began. The high water level meant that most of the hides were remote from dry land and, whereas those fowlers with the foresight to have donned thigh waders were able to avoid wet feet, the few wearing wellingtons had to reconcile themselves to a soaking. The problems of the fowlers, however, were slight compared to those encountered by our dogs. While I discovered that to lower my head below the top of the hide entailed crouching in such a fashion that my backside became submerged, Meg was committed to an hour of swimming in circles. Although a cold, wet bottom did nothing to improve the standard of my shooting, I fear that the effect of circular paddling had disastrous consequences for my labrador's interest in the sport. The poor beast was too busy keeping her head above water to mark any bird which was shot - and those were few and far between.

Around the loch the same story was emerging. Guns were unable to get cover or reasonable shooting stances and the odd duck which was sufficiently unlucky to collide with a charge of shot was left unmarked, to be searched for at the end of the shoot. Despite our high expectations, the bag at the end of the day consisted of 3 tufties, a mallard and a shoveler. Fortunately wildfowlers are not easily daunted by adverse conditions so, as dogs and clothing were dried in the lodge, the conversation turned to the remaining two months of the season and the sport which surely lay ahead.

A fortnight later we returned with hopes renewed. The water level had dropped to near normal and conditions looked perfect for a splendid flight. Well before daybreak, nine men were ensconced in their hides, dogs were sitting high and dry on the fish boxes which we had brought down during the week, full cartridge bags hung inside the butts and we awaited the arrival of the quarry. We waited .... and waited. Eventually, a good hour after dawn, the first shots were fired from the east end of the loch. Just as Meg looked at me as if to ask what anyone was finding to shoot at, a pair of mallard suddenly flashed past slightly out of range. The dog's eyes followed them as they circled the water, doubtlessly hoping that they might come back round. It was not to be. A shot rang out from a neighbouring hide and the drake tumbled out of the sky while his mate made herself scarce in the direction of the sun. At 10 o'clock we persuaded ourselves that no more duck were coming and stood back to admire the morning's bag of 2 teal and the single mallard.

So was set the pattern for the rest of the season. The keener members of the party continued to arrive at unearthly hours of the morning to be ferried out to hides and await the flight which never materialised. There were duck frequenting the loch - a few mallard one week, a dozen teal the next; a pair of goldeneye on one occasion and, twice, a small flock of greylag driven off the foreshore by storm-force winds. But never the prodigious stock of birds which had initially lured us to the water.

When January drew to a close the consensus of opinion was that our club had wasted its money and a decision was taken to terminate the lease. Not being convinced that the water had been afforded a fair trial, I arranged for my own name to be substituted as tenant and, accompanied by a group of friends, spent the following autumn and winter critically examining the comings and goings - principally the goings - of the fowl on the loch. Their numbers seemed slightly higher than we had encountered during the previous season but sport continued to be somewhat sparse.

The highlight of that year occurred in early November. I had invited WAGBI (as it then was) to base a wildfowling course at the loch and a morning flight was arranged as part of the curriculum. For once fate was kind and, although the bag was not enormous, our students succeeded in shooting an interesting variety of duck. Mallard, teal, pochard, goldeneye, tufted duck and gadwall were proudly carried back to the hotel to augment the specimens for a wildfowl identification session later in the day. A useful bonus from that course derived from the fact that veteran fowlers Arthur Cadman and Allan Allison were amongst the lecturers and each was able to offer constructive advice regarding potential improvements to the shoot.

Throughout the following summer we worked to put a fresh management plan into operation. New hides were required in different positions so trailer loads of timber pallets were unloaded at strategic points. Whoever invented the fork-lift truck certainly rendered a considerable service to wildfowling. Never had hides been constructed so rapidly nor so solidly before the advent of the ubiquitous pallet. As a fiery August came to its end we witnessed an unprecedented number of mallard frequenting the water and a few families of teal appeared to have bred successfully in the vicinity.

It was, therefore, with renewed optimism that a breezy group of fowlers arrived for the first shoot of the new season. The effervescent mood of the party belied the fact that each had risen from his bed before 4 o'clock and anticipation was heightened when the fishery manager reported that a steady build-up of duck had continued throughout the first fortnight of September.

In contrast to previous flights on the loch there was no anticlimax that morning, no let-down as dawn came and went. Only one Gun failed to score but even he saw enough action to have made his journey worthwhile. The bag was by no means fantastic but it did demonstrate that careful thought and some hard work were necessary prerequisites of successful sport on that loch. Lessons had been learned the hard way and unrealistic expectations tempered. Perseverance had not only shown us how to shoot the loch to maximum advantage; those who possessed the resolve to stay the course had also learned how to gain satisfaction from moderate sport coupled with a greater involvement in the management of the shoot. Instead of going out weighed down with 50 cartridges, we settled for carrying a pocketful of ammunition together with a bag of tools to repair or improve our hides.

A few years later, also in mid-season, the wildfowling club had an amazing stroke of luck when an opportunity arose to rent some shooting rights adjacent to Loch Leven. Frequently, when motoring south with empty bags from a sortie to one of the estuaries, Leon and I cast covetous glances at the great flocks of geese grazing in the stubbles alongside the motorway or filling the sky as they moved from field to field in search of the richest feeding. We knew that the loch itself was a nature reserve and that the estate which surrounded it was so carefully managed that no itinerant fowler was likely to be permitted to set foot on its verdant pastures.

What we did not realise at that time was that a small section of the loch's shoreline was in independent ownership. It was a vigilant club secretary who noticed a small advertisement in the local newspaper offering the sporting lease of a single field which ran down to the water's edge. A letter was written, an interview arranged and it said a good deal about the reputation of the club when, from over 100 applicants, the landowner chose us to be his shooting tenants.

Needless to say, the responsibilities placed upon the shoulders of the club committee were enormous. Under the watchful eyes of the nature reserve warden and the keepers of the adjoining estate, no lapse of good conduct could be permitted nor any hint of greed be tolerated. Fully aware of the burden resting upon its membership, the committee drew up a rota which ensured that both the frequency of shooting and the number of Guns were strictly controlled.

It was under this arrangement that, with considerable excitement, I prepared for my first flight at the loch. Days of rain had transformed the landscape into a patchwork of flood and flash while the temperature plummeted to deliver a final deathblow to the Korean chrysanthemums in the garden. From my window I could see that the first snow of winter had capped the hills and I retired to bed on the night before the flight with modest optimism for the morrow.

As always on shooting days, I awoke long before the alarm clock disturbed the rest of the household and washing, shaving, breakfasting and dressing were performed in a most perfunctory fashion. My mind was firmly on the hours ahead - a preoccupation which, judging from the scuffles emitting from the kennel outside, was shared by the labradors. As gun, clothing and dogs were packed into the Land-Rover, I noted that not only had the wind of the previous evening dropped to a gentle breeze but, perversely, the clouds had cleared during the night and a full moon brightly illuminated the snowy hilltops. Such conditions inevitably spell disaster for a morning flight on the estuary so I feared that the geese on the loch might already have deserted the roost to feed in the silver moonlight.

In the event, I need not have worried. I met the other two Guns who were scheduled to shoot that morning and we walked down the long narrow field to an accompaniment of goose music from many, many geese out on the water. Although the eastern sky was tinged with only the merest hint of dawn, the grey flocks were clearly preening in preparation for another day. We each ensconced ourselves in the tangle of reeds, rushes and hawthorn which lined the shore and slipped cartridges into the chambers of our guns in readiness for the flight.

Duck began to move very early. From my own position I was unable to catch sight of them until they had cleared the black backdrop of trees behind me and most were well out of shot before the gun could be brought to shoulder. A single bird did, however, give an advance warning quack and paid the price for its noisy approach. At last the pinkfeet and greylag began to grow restless. First a few small skeins rose from the vicinity of the long island and traversed the length of the loch to pass high over the lights of a nearby town. For a period of 20 minutes the activity increased until the sky seemed full of geese - skeins large and small, orderly and ragged, silent and calling, high and low. But only the high ones, it seemed, came over our field. There were a few to which guns were raised but, discretion prevailing, triggers were not pulled. The possibility that a warden might have had his field glasses trained upon us added an extra margin of caution to our range-judging.

When we reckoned that the flight had ended we gathered by the boundary river to discuss the prospects for the remainder of the season. Certainly harder weather was required and a good gale would not go amiss. We were earnestly considering whether an evening duck flight might pay dividends when a loud "wink-wink-wink" caused us to dodge behind a thorny briar. Being the only one who had not slipped his gun into its cover, the youngest member of the party hurriedly thrust a single cartridge into the chamber of his 20-bore and brought the gun to bear upon the leader of four pinkfeet which had caught us unawares as they flighted the wrong way back towards the loch. As so often happens with a snap shot, his aim was spot-on and the goose tumbled out of the sky stone-dead. For once Meg did not run in and I was able to send my younger dog over the wide stream to collect the bird.

While we were watching her swim back, another small group of pinks emerged from behind the trees and passed directly overhead well within range. This time no-one succeeded in getting a cartridge into his gun.

Sadly, as the years passed, the number of club members who were willing to pay a small additional subscription for the privilege of shooting at the Big Loch declined and a few of us were fortunate in persuading the landowner to make a private arrangement for a continued lease. Admittedly, having access to only a few hundred yards of the loch's 12-mile shoreline means that the geese do not always flight over our patch but, when the weather is suitably wild, watching the great skeins battle against a gale as they come off that expansive inland water is the next best thing to being far out on the foreshore.

Wildfowling below the sea wall is essentially a solitary occupation. Shooting duck or geese inland, on the other hand, can have its social side and, occasionally, the pursuit of fowl might be coupled with a few hours of roughshooting.

Just such a day of mixed sport resulted from a telephone call from Patrick Keen who, at that time, was a director of one of Britain's largest shotgun distributors. He had, a year earlier, provided me with a new gun to test for one of the shooting magazines and suggested that I returned it to his Perthshire retreat one Saturday morning. There followed an invitation to arrive sufficiently early to have a crack at the geese which frequented the loch near his cottage.

Patrick's directions were easily followed and I located his hideaway without difficulty. Then, over a very welcome cup of coffee, I was introduced to fellow guests Johnny and Angus and to Caroline who most efficiently combined the roles of cook, driver and official photographer.

The value of reconnaissance and preparation for a goose foray cannot be overstated but Patrick took the matter to an extreme of thoroughness. Setting up a large scale map on an easel he explained that, while he was away on business, Caroline had spent her mornings crawling along ditches to check up on the movements of the geese. The positions for each Gun were marked on the map as the plan of campaign unfolded. Greylag would make a short flight from the loch to a nearby grass field, Patrick asserted, and would do so in skeins of 20 to 30 birds. Any shots fired at that stage would disturb the geese still on the loch and send them off in the opposite direction.

The strategy, therefore, was to take our places while it was still dark and lie low until all the birds were feeding on the pasture. When he adjudged the time to be right, Patrick would fire a single shot into the air and, if the scheme worked, the greys would take to the sky and flight over the waiting Guns. It was absolutely forbidden for anyone to pull a trigger until the signal had been given. On many previous occasions I had heard a similar plan related by a hopeful host and I knew only too well that the geese usually had other intentions. To observe the common courtesies demanded of a guest, however, I resolved to abide by his instructions.

After a short drive in the Land-Rover we disembarked in the darkness beside some farm buildings. The sound of the greylag on the roost served to quicken our steps as we headed for the appointed field where I was dropped off in a ditch on the southern boundary while the others crossed to the opposite side. Barely 10 minutes passed before the calling of geese in flight rose above the general music of preening birds.

My gutter was half-filled with flood water yet, to avoid being seen, I was forced to crouch low with my face practically pressed into the mud. In the semi-darkness I risked an occasional furtive glance over the top to watch small groups of greys circling the field before pitching confidently into the centre. Now and then a party would pass directly overhead, not more than 20 yards high, and if the itching of my trigger finger was difficult to quell, preventing Moy's eagerness from giving the game away was even more problematic. Almost half an hour elapsed before the stream of geese from the loch showed any sign of abating, by which time well over a thousand birds were grazing contentedly on the lush grass.

Some of the greys were within six feet of my ditch and, through the stalks of herbage, I surveyed the scene with amazement. Never before had I been so close to unsuspecting geese. The noise from the great flock was overpowering. Angus later described it as being akin to the buzzing of a billion butch bees and I was hard pressed to think of a more appropriate phrase. Moy grew increasingly excited as the noise level increased and, in the end, I had to lie firmly on top of the poor labrador to prevent her from sticking her head up for a better view.

Suddenly the sound of a single shot rang out from across the field and the busy murmuring of the feeding birds abruptly changed to the roar of threshing pinions and then into the cacophonous flight call of a huge flock of greylag. Up the pasture they swept, rising into the wind. At the head of the meadow the birds turned and. still gaining height, flighted back towards our positions in several long ragged skeins. Without any conscious decision I sprang up, threw the gun to my shoulder and, just as I realised that my feet were firmly stuck in the mud in the bottom of the ditch, pulled the trigger. The goose at which I had fired thumped into the grass at exactly the same instant as I landed on my back in the water. If I had possessed sufficient presence of mind I might have been able to take a semi-submerged second shot to complete the right-and-left but I have to confess that the thought never entered my head.

Taking the bird from Moy, I crossed the field to where Angus was picking up another grey. Soon we were joined by Johnny, also proudly bearing a goose, and we spent a few moments remarking upon the wonder and excitement of the occasion. When a gooseless Patrick strode into sight the injustice was obvious. After planning the campaign so perfectly, he had failed to score. Then, as if to ensure fair play, a single greylag called from high above the trees. Patrick's gun went up and the goose came down.

Angus had to leave at that point so, after Caroline had taken a couple of photographs for the record book, she added the role of beater to her varied repertoire of skills and accompanied the remaining three Guns for an impromptu walk around the few hundred acres of farmland over which Patrick had permission to shoot.

We crossed a narrow wooden bridge and lined up to walk through an area of rough grazing. Towards the end of that field we came to a dry-stane dyke and, as was her wont, Moy trotted forward and placed her front paws atop the stones to view the land on the other side. As she surveyed the vista, a covey of five or six partridge rose from the shelter of the wall and whirred away from us. Once more I was denied a right-and-left. My first shot brought down two of the little brown birds and such was my surprise that I forgot a second barrel was available.

A short drive through a field of turnips brought a pheasant and another partridge to Johnny and then we crossed a small paddock at the top end of the shoot. Over a barbed wire fence lay a little triangle of rough grass and whin bushes through which we would have to pass before reaching another area of turnips. We were all astride the wire, guns correctly unloaded, when a strong covey of partridge erupted from the base of a clump of whins and escaped, unsaluted, over the field. A few mild expletives were exchanged but we had not altered our stances when a single partridge took wing from the same bush and followed its fellows over the horizon.

Quickly we untangled ourselves from the fence, reloaded our weapons and sent the dogs forward with a faint hope that yet another perdix might be lurking in the cover. Instead of a partridge, however, Moy nosed a large cock pheasant which rocketed skywards, protesting noisily. My shot stopped it dead and, at the report of the gun, a rabbit and a big brown hare fled from the whins. Patrick accounted for the bunny. Next, Caroline and Patrick drove a sloping field of turnips which yielded three pheasant, all of them superbly grown wild birds. Finally, heading back towards the rickety timber bridge, Patrick placed the efficacy of his little 20-bore beyond doubt by taking a right-and-left from a covey of partridge which appeared but fleetingly before disappearing into a tall stand of trees.

Fifteen minutes later we unloaded four geese, five pheasant, six partridge and the solitary rabbit from the Land-Rover and retired into the house for a gargantuan meal of porridge, bacon, eggs, tomatoes, mushrooms and black pudding. I was halfway through a huge plateful of the delicious fry-up before I looked at my wristwatch and discovered that it was only 10.45 am.

Decoying geese on inland stubbles is a subject which never ceases to arouse a great deal of emotive controversy whenever wildfowlers debate the ethics of their sport. There is no doubt that excessive numbers of wildfowl can be killed by unscrupulous shooters when decoys are employed and, as dead wild geese cannot legally be sold, there is never any excuse for shooting large bags of those magnificent birds. When practised with restraint, however, attempting to lure pinkfeet or greylag into gunshot range by the use of calls and decoys can be a challenging and satisfying branch of the sport.

One fowling guide who became noted for insisting that his clients stopped shooting after three or four geese had been shot was Mal Kempston. He operated in an area not far from my home and, once or twice each season, he used to invite me to accompany him on a dawn outing. The pleasure of such mornings lay not only in having the opportunity to shoot a goose or two but, more particularly, in witnessing a master at work. Not that the geese invariably co-operated!

It was a thoroughly miserable day to be engaged in any pursuit other than fowling. Torrential rain had fallen throughout the night and my 10 mile drive had to be taken with the utmost caution to avoid the deep flood water under which several sections of the road were submerged. Doubtlessly the local authority would have its standby squads out to clear blocked drains long before the commuter traffic took to the highways but, at 5.30 am, I passed several stranded motor cars on my journey to meet Mal at the hotel from which he worked.

When I drew up in the car park the rain had abated to a persistent drizzle. Under the street lights I was introduced to the two Irishmen who would be shooting that morning and I nodded sagely as Mal recited his ritual briefing. No guns were to be loaded until the hides had been built and decoys set out. The geese should be allowed to circle until they were within easy range and no-one must shoot until he gave the word. Whatever the outcome, we would leave the fields by 9 o'clock in order that the birds might be allowed to settle and enjoy a full day's feeding without harassment. His lecture concluded, our guide then climbed into his van and led the small convoy eastwards.

At the farm we parked in an extremely muddy field where, our boots squelching in a veritable quagmire, four bulky sacks were unloaded from Mal's vehicle and hoisted on to our shoulders. Thus laden, it was necessary to cross two fields of barley stubble and one of soft rutted plough before reaching the place where geese had been feeding the day before. Only a wire strand fence gave any semblance of cover so the first task was to unpack camouflage netting from one of the sacks and drape it over the wire. To give our hide a more natural appearance, armfuls of straw-coloured grass were piled against the base of the netting and a few tufts woven into the mesh to break up the uniformity of its outline.

One of the other sacks contained half a dozen full-bodied plastic geese while the remaining two held 40 lightweight shell decoys. Under Mal's instruction we placed those out on the barley stubble in an irregular pattern, taking care to ensure that the majority faced into the wind. Some wildfowlers believe that they can make do with 10 or 12 decoys but most professional guides consider that a much larger number is required to give a realistic impression of a feeding flock. Certainly, as we climbed over the fence and crouched down behind our camouflaged hide, the spread of surrogate geese before us looked exceedingly lifelike.

While we patiently waited in the murky dawn, the Irish fowlers told tales of flighting whitefronted geese on the Wexford Slobs and shooting mallard, goldeneye and pochard beside Lough Sheelin. Then, from far away in the grey morning sky, we picked up the faint music of pinkfeet. Mal put his wooden goose call to his lips and began to talk to the, as yet, invisible skein. Peering through the mesh of the netting we scanned the horizon as the sound of the pinks grew in intensity. At last, through the mist and drizzle, a wavering line of around 30 birds emerged and the master changed the notes from his call to produce the low, chattering murmur of feeding geese. Lower and lower came the pinkfeet, circling the field once, twice and then a third time. They were obviously interested in the decoys but hesitated to approach too close. On their fourth circuit we thought that the birds were about to alight amidst their plastic lookalikes but, while still over the centre of the stubble field, the leader wiffled from the sky and the others followed to land 150 yards from our fence.

That is just about the worst thing that can happen when decoying. During the next half-hour three more skeins of pinks approached but, try as he might with his call, Mal could not persuade them to come to our decoys in preference to the ever-increasing flock of real geese in the middle of the field. Eventually, true to his word, the guide announced that it was 9 o'clock and we drew stumps without having fired a shot. Naturally, when the decoys were collected and hides dismantled, the feeding pinks lifted from the stubble. As we trudged back towards the cars the geese were still circling high overhead and, before we drove away, they had dropped back into the field to pick waste grain from amongst the harvested stalks.

Over a hearty breakfast in the hotel a post-mortem was held. Were the decoys a trifle too close to the fence? Had we interwoven enough grass into the netting? Might the rain have caused the plastic shells to shine despite Mal's care in painting them with a matt finish? Definitive answers could not be found but the visitors from Ireland were already eagerly anticipating the next morning when, perhaps, a change of strategy might bring the geese within range.

Chapter 5

Dogs and Guns

Far out on the marsh an occasional gabble of goose talk could just be heard above the unceasing howl of a late November gale. The eastern sky wanted to lighten but, for almost an hour, dawn fought a losing battle against louring black clouds which scudded across the heavens in the teeth of the tempest. With Moy trying to coorie close for shelter, I crouched in the parsimonious lee of a shallow gully hoping that, on this morning of all mornings, the pinkfeet might revert to their old flightline. Twenty years earlier I could have been sure that, on just such a day, the geese would rise from their roost and follow the course of the river channel but, due to greatly increased shooting pressure in recent times, their behaviour had become much less predictable.

The reason for so badly wanting to be under the pinks that morning was cradled lovingly in my lap. Instead of being armed with my familiar Beretta, I had chosen the first real storm of the season to take out the larger of two guns which Patrick Keen had entrusted to my tender care for a couple of months. With its massive 44" barrel, the 4-bore by E.M. Reilly would be utterly wasted on any quarry other than foreshore geese so I prayed that the great grey birds would favour me with an opportunity to use it.

In the darkness a party of wigeon streaked over with the wind in their tails. Under other circumstances I might have risked a snap shot at their fleeting forms as, in such wild conditions, the report of a gun would not disturb the pinkfeet which still paddled on the distant mudflats. With only two cartridges at my disposal, however, there was no way in which I was going to waste almost a quarter pound of lead on mere duck. Even Moy seemed to understand and I was spared the reproachful glance which she normally cast in my direction if she felt that a good chance had been allowed to pass.

Eventually the geese decided that they could wait no longer for sunrise. The first few groups lifted from the mud and headed along the shore before turning to cross the sea wall half a mile to the west. Then the main body of the flock rose into the sky and sorted itself out into several ragged skeins which battled landwards against the raging storm. For a few moments I gripped the gun tighter, watching the nearest geese as they seemed to come in my direction. But, before the birds reached my gully, they wheeled right and passed 100 yards along the shore.

Several little parties of stragglers came close before turning to follow the path of their fellows and I feared that my journey had been in vain. I was on the point of removing the 4" cartridge from the chamber of the mighty gun when Moy's tail began to thump against my wadered leg. Looking seawards I saw a pair of pinks over the turbulent brown water of the river channel. In almost every branch of shooting sport the enjoyment to be derived from the pursuit is greatly enhanced when each Gun is accompanied by a well trained gundog. Wherever shooting men or women gather, it is almost inevitable that, sooner or later, the conversation will drift towards the subject of dogs and tales will be told of brilliant canine companions which possess powers well beyond those normally attributed to any dumb animal. Alternatively, the stories may centre upon less virtuous gundogs - always belonging to other people - which have committed the most atrocious misdemeanours.

The relationship between man and dog is an integral part of the shooting scene and nowhere is it more intense than on a wild marsh at morning flight. When waiting patiently for the first pale grey streaks of dawn to herald the start of another day, when listening to the murmuring of wakening geese far out on the remote saltings, when sheltering from the cruel fury of a midwinter storm, then is the companionship of a faithful retriever most valued. When, after that long vigil, a shot duck or goose drops into fast-flowing water, the ability of a good gundog to swim strongly and pick the bird is absolutely indispensable.

Meg was a thickset black labrador which really lived for wildfowling. In her later years, if put into a pheasant covert, she would have cleared the wood of birds in minutes or, should a hare have risen in front of her nose while walking-up partridge, it would have been coursed into the next county. Her faults were, of course, due entirely to shortcomings on my part. Having read all of the books on gundog training, I tutored the little bitch through her puppyhood and then, delighted with the results, became complacent. Her skills thereafter developed by chance rather than by design so that, after a few seasons of steady all-round work, she grew less reliable in the game shooting field but graduated to become an absolute mistress of the saltmarsh.

There is undoubtedly a considerable element of chance involved in the acquisition of any gundog puppy. Essential features such as a good nose and soft mouth are probably genetically determined and, without those inborn attributes, no amount of careful training will produce a worthwhile retriever.

Fortunately, Meg had an exceptional sense of smell and, so gentle was she when carrying any object in her mouth, she could be sent to pick up an egg and would deliver it to hand unbroken. Her senses of sight and hearing also were quite remarkable so that, all in all, the qualities which enabled her to perform such outstanding service on more than 600 fowling expeditions had little to do with my own early attempts at gundog training.

On occasions without number, while waiting expectantly for the pinkfeet to rise from their roost, Meg's keen ears would pick up the first strains of goose music from the distant heavens and the wagging of her thick tail was the signal to grip the gun a little tighter. When cosily ensconced in a deep gutter, she would sit facing me, her sharp eyes constantly scanning the dark sky over my shoulder. Time and time again she froze to attention and gave an unfailing warning of mallard approaching silently from behind. And then, if the shot was successful, she would be off to collect the slain quarry, her nose leading her to the fallen bird with unerring accuracy.

Where the dunes narrow and meet the shore of the outer estuary, a little reed-fringed depression in the sand fills with water at each tide. One morning, many years ago, two members of the wildfowling club arrived at the spot and discovered more than 200 geese having a wash and brush-up in the shallows. Although the phenomenon was never repeated, that small tidal lake became known as the "goose pool".

The sandhills overlooking the pool provided an ideal hiding place for a waiting gunner and, if the pinks were roosting far out on the flats, their flightline might be directly over his head.

With that possibility in mind, I had risen very early and taken Meg from her kennel. Under the harsh sodium lights of the quiet village streets nothing moved and we travelled eastwards along deserted country roads. In the market town the first signs of a new day were beginning to show. A squad of cleaning ladies waited for the caretaker to open up the ancient oak doors of the school and a mailvan stood outside the post office, its exhaust billowing white in the cold morning air. Another few miles of empty highways and then we met a sudden flurry of activity as the nightshift spilled out of the mill at the head of the river.

Turning down the narrow forest track it was with an element of selfish satisfaction that I noted no other tyre marks in the glistening covering of hoar frost. Around the gamekeeper's cottage sleepy pheasants perched in the conifers like fairy lights on a Christmas tree but those birds aroused no sense of excitement on a morning when the pursuit of a nobler quarry was in prospect.

Stars still twinkled brightly in the clear black sky as I released Meg from the back of the car and swiftly climbed into overtrousers, wellingtons and a warm camouflaged jacket. Then, checking that there was an ample supply of cartridges in my pocket and that the car doors were securely locked, I whistled the dog to heel and strode out along the well-worn path through the dunes towards the shore. Only the merest breeze ruffled the long coarse grass and, with the better part of a mile still to walk, the faint strains of goose talk greeted my ears.

Spurred on by the welcome sound, I hastened my pace and allowed Meg to hunt ahead as we progressed. Twice she put up rabbits from in front of her nose and stood, stock still, watching them bolt. The thought may have been entirely fanciful but I credited the fact that she did not give chase, as she normally would have done, to some knowledge on her part about the real purpose of the outing.

When, at last, the goose pool was reached, I crept cautiously over the sand to find a hiding place in the reed fringes. The eastern sky was just beginning to take on an indigo hue as, with Meg now keeping very close, I settled down to await dawn. Although the pinkfeet were fully 400 yards out on the flats, their music seemed to surround me and, anticipating an excellent flight, I guessed that there must be upwards of 1000 birds on the roost.

Without a strong wind or stormy sea to disturb their leisure, the geese were in no hurry to leave the foreshore that morning. Ever so slowly the world lightened and the estuary came awake. The first birds to move were herring gulls which travelled silently landwards, no doubt to seek out and follow an early tractor ploughing the barley stubbles. Then, singly and in pairs, crows descended upon the shoreline, their raucous cawing rudely disturbing the tranquil scene as they searched for morsels amongst the seaweed at high water mark. When the golden orb of the sun poked above the far horizon, woodpigeon came out from the forest and dropped down to the sands to replenish the supply of grit in their crops before departing inland again for their breakfast.

Still the pinkfeet did not move. At one stage a sudden movement of Meg's head caused me to look behind and I simultaneously sank lower into the reeds and gripped the gun tighter as three long-necked shapes registered on the periphery of my vision. Before the safety catch had been slipped forward, however, the birds revealed themselves as cormorants. How often, I wondered, had those evil-looking fisheaters caused a wildfowler's pulse to quicken in vain?

I remembered other mornings when, under similar conditions, it had been a full hour after sunrise before the geese rose from the shore. My vigil that day might have been equally protracted had not a helicopter from the nearby airfield appeared in the sky. It is a strange matter that the fowl are able to ignore jet fighters streaking over their heads but become greatly disturbed if a whirlybird approaches within half a mile. Protesting noisily, the huge flock took to the air and, like a dense dark cloud, headed low over the sand towards me.

Conscious of the adrenalin affecting my heart-rate, I crouched low, trying desperately to attain invisibility in my sparse reed haven. Then everything seemed to go wrong. With the first birds directly overhead, I sprang up and pulled the trigger. Missed! Swinging on to another goose I pulled again but the firing pin fell impotently on to the primer and the cartridge did not detonate. Birds were streaming over my position as I fumbled to remove the dud shell and insert another round into the upper chamber of my gun but, in my haste, I dropped the cartridge into the water at my feet.

By the time that I had succeeded in reloading, the skein was well out of range and I muttered a string of curses at the lost opportunity. Then I noticed that Meg's eyes were still firmly fixed on the departing pinks and, following the direction of her gaze, I saw one of the birds falter and begin to lose height. Without waiting for a command, the little bitch took off and raced out of sight into the sand dunes. She was away for fully 10 minutes and I had removed the cartridges from the gun, buckled it into its sleeve and was considering whether to set out in search of her when she re-appeared over the crest of the nearest dune, clutching the fat goose in her tender jaws. It is a cardinal rule of wildfowling that, whenever one appears to suffer an inexplicable miss, the birds should be watched vigilantly until they are out of sight. A wounded goose can carry on flying for a considerable distance before dropping from the skein and, if it has been hit, every effort must be made to retrieve it. That morning, in my dejection, I had failed to abide by the rule but Meg saved both the day and the bird.

Meg was turning decidedly grey around the muzzle when Moy arrived upon the scene. The younger, slimmer bitch was entirely different in almost every respect and, from the beginning, demonstrated the potential to become and remain a top class gundog. Admittedly I took considerably greater care with her training but this was aided by a degree of overt dependence whereby her whole life, outside the kennel, was dedicated to pleasing her lord and master. Although her temperament in this respect was a huge bonus when shooting grouse or pheasant, it had a number of disadvantages below the sea wall. For example, while patiently awaiting morning flight, she spent her time watching me rather than scanning the sky for approaching duck. Only when a shot was fired would her eyes turn to mark down the falling bird and then, unlike Meg, she remained rock steady until sent to retrieve.

Despite Meg's advancing age there was a period of several years when both labradors accompanied me on fowling expeditions. If either Peter or Leon came along, bringing their own dogs, then the pack of black labs present would frequently exceed the number of duck or geese to be retrieved.

During this time we tended to favour the north shore of one of the larger estuaries and, although the trip entailed a fairly long drive, there were few Saturday mornings when Leon, with Foss occupying most of the space in the rear of his van, did not pick me up at some really unearthly hour. I very much doubt if dogs relate to each other in the same way as people do but, on those early morning forays, it always seemed that Meg and Foss were the closest of friends while Moy remained aloof, appearing to prefer human company.

Some of those mornings were spent at a spot halfway along the shore of the Firth where a public road ran down almost to the water's edge. Cars could be parked close to a small natural harbour and fowlers would walk along the top of the broad sea wall in either direction to find a hiding place in the dense belt of reeds which lined high water mark. In many respects this was "tame" wildfowling as it was very common to return from a flight without ever having stepped on to soft mud nor crawled along a flooded gutter. The attraction of that place derived not only from the ease of access but also from the fact that, a few hundred yards offshore, lay several long mudbanks which were covered by only the highest spring tides. If undisturbed, geese would roost on those banks and, when flighting off at dawn, might pass over the grassy sea wall just within shotgun range.

It is tempting, years later, to look back on those days with a measure of disdain, feeling perhaps that wilder opportunities to do business with the fowl should have been sought. They were, however, pleasant outings during which there was much to be seen. While seated comfortably against a banking, sheltered from the wind, wrens, goldcrests and a variety of tits might be watched as they flitted amongst the swaying stalks of the high reeds. In midwinter, when natural feeding was scarce, those tiny birds lost all caution and would come within a few feet of an armed wildfowler to hungrily devour a carelessly dropped sandwich crumb or other titbit. As daylight strengthened, great flocks of fieldfares swooped low over the foreshore, their "chack-chack" calls mingling with the whoosh of a thousand wings. Sometimes teal might unwittingly drop into the ditch which ran behind the sea wall and then, discovering that they had unwelcome human company, spring vertically into the air to effect their escape. Little did those diminutive duck know that, although only a few yards above high water mark, they were safe from the guns of shore-bound fowlers. Less secure were the pheasants which occasionally strayed from the adjacent estate on to the shore. Much to the chagrin of the laird's gamekeeper, as soon as his precious charges crossed the tideline, they became legitimate quarry and, on mornings when the greylag skeins had passed too high or too wide, consolation might be obtained in the form of an errant longtail.

Unfortunately, but perhaps inevitably, the lure of the geese roosting on the mudbanks grew too tempting for some fowlers and it became common practice for boats to be taken out before dawn from the town on the south shore of the estuary. Then, instead of the chirping of small birds and the piping of waders, the early morning silence was rudely broken by the sound of outboard motors revving in mid-channel. Not surprisingly, the area was soon forsaken by the geese and, to the best of my knowledge, they have not returned to that part of the Firth in the numbers which Leon and I used to see.

Knowing that the great grey flocks were still in the general vicinity, we explored farther east and eventually discovered that the greylag were frequenting the wide mudflats of a large bay some seven miles along the shore. The terrain was so treacherous that, at low tide, no-one could approach within three-quarters of a mile of the roost and, in those circumstances, only a force-8 gale would cause the birds to remain within gunshot range as they flighted inland to feed. For this reason we normally timed our visits to coincide with a flowing tide in the hope that the greys would begin their daily journey from a point closer to the narrow belt of saltmarsh which skirted the shoreline. That bay was the scene of one of the few sorties when the services of Meg, Moy and Foss were required simultaneously.

Pulling in to a disused farm track, Leon switched off the engine of his rusting van and, immediately, we could hear the calling of greylag close to hand. Despite the sky still being pitch black, we feared that the geese might flight early so, without wasting any time, we donned our thigh waders and waxproofs and hurried down to the foreshore.

It was a bitterly cold January morning with the merest smattering of powdery snow clinging to each blade of grass on the hard, rutted marsh. Even where the tide had washed only a few hours earlier, the penetrating chill of midwinter had crispened the surface of the saltings so that each footstep crunched in the darkness. Drawn ever onwards by the anserine chorus, we at last found our progress blocked by the deep gully of a stream which meandered parallel to the sea wall before turning out to join the waters of the estuary. Knowing that the flock of greylag was not more than 300 yards in front, we sought cover in the reeded verges of the little river and settled down to await the coming of daylight.

Despite two layers of thick thermal stockings my feet were soon numb with the cold and my beard grew brittle as condensation froze in it at every breath. When a yellow and purple false dawn changed, quite abruptly, to the weak pinks and blues of a new morning the temperature seemed to drop a few more degrees and I began to have a serious concern that my fingers might be incapable of operating the safety catch and trigger of my gun.

Happily the geese did not tarry unduly on the shore that day. Well before sunrise they grew restless and, perhaps spurred into early flight by the sub-zero conditions, rose from the frozen mudflats in a single skein which came towards us fast and low. Because the long line of greys was little more than 20 yards high, it was possible for the shots to be taken while they were still well out in front. Presented with such an ideal opportunity, no mistakes were made and Leon and I were rewarded with one of the very rare achievements of a right-and-left each. Indeed, I cannot think of any other morning when we concurrently scored a double.

One of my birds dropped into the water of the stream while the other three fell on the far side of the gully. Without waiting to be sent, Meg lept into the river and, pushing iceflows aside with her muzzle, paddled out to collect the floating greylag. I sent Moy to pick my other goose and, as she swam across towards the opposite bank, I noticed that Foss was already preparing to re-enter the water with the first of Leon's birds in his mouth.

Its amazing how jubilation banishes discomfort. Once all four geese had been retrieved, we stood for several minutes discussing the flight and scanning the distant mud for any sign of more fowl before turning to leave the marsh. That was when we became aware that, instead of three black labradors, we were accompanied by dogs which had turned white. Millions of tiny ice crystals sparkled in their thick coats yet they did not appear to be in the least troubled by their condition. It is little wonder that labradors are so popular as wildfowling dogs - their evolution in the arduous climate of Newfoundland has fitted them perfectly to cope with the extremes of our own winters.

The next few years witnessed a marked expansion of my kennel. Moy produced an excellent litter of pups, two if which - Flight and Teal - remained with me until their training was complete and gave a great deal of pleasure before going off to work for other sportsmen. Another of that litter, Spartan Lady, was trained by Jim Munro to achieve high honours in the field trial world, including two remarkable performances in the British Retriever Championship. Much as I enjoyed putting young dogs through their schooling, however, I never seemed to have time to become personally involved in competitive activity. My principal criterion for judging a labrador remained its prowess on the wild marsh.

A north-easterly blast almost took my breath away as I stepped out of the house into the wintry blackness and crossed to the kennel. Moy was in season so, rather than risk any unwelcome encounters with canine males, I opted to take Meg out on her own. The destination was a point on the south shore of the estuary where, according to local rumour, there might be a chance of getting under a smallish flock of greylag.

It was still very dark when we arrived and despite her 14 years, Meg transmitted obvious signs of pleasure at being out and about before dawn although, as we walked down the grass track towards the shore, she stayed closer to heel than normal.

"You're slowing down, old girl," I told her, remembering the many mornings a decade earlier when I was happy to see her coursing through the long grass, chasing rabbit scents and running off her surplus energy before squatting down for a long wait on the saltings.

We found a likely spot near the river channel and built a low wall of seaweed behind which to hide. Wigeon were whistling as they passed unseen against the inky firmament and, once or twice, the single quack of a mallard brought the elderly labrador to rigid attention. Just as the sky was beginning to turn that apple green hue which so often precedes a winter dawn, I noted two other fowlers moving into position a couple of hundred yards to the east.

Almost an hour elapsed before the greys which were roosting out on the mudflats decided to move. With my face pressed close to the odorous weed, I watched them follow the course of the river and then wheel south while still out of range of my hide. Then two shots sounded over the estuary and one bird fell from the skein, dead in the air.

As it was reasonably certain that no more geese remained on the shore I picked up my bag and walked over to greet the other men. The tide had been flowing steadily throughout our time on the marsh and I found the two fowlers standing at what was, in effect, the edge of the North Sea. It transpired that they were father and son and it was the younger, a lad of about 16, who had shot the greylag. Unfortunately the bird had dropped into the river, had floated downstream and was now bobbing in the waves a good 50 yards away.

Doubting if Meg would be able to see the goose floating low in the water, I put a cartridge into the lower chamber of my Beretta and fired it in the general direction of the dead bird. The old dog required no second telling - she took to the sea and swam out for 20 or 30 yards before looking back for a directional signal. A wave of my left arm sent her on the correct course and she soon spotted the goose, made straight for it and, as she had done dozens of times before, scooped it into her jaws as she turned back towards the shore.

I watched anxiously as she appeared to make rather heavier weather than normal of the return journey for I knew that, having picked the bird, she would drown before she would let it go. Eventually she reached dry land and placed the greylag at my feet before shaking herself. The young lad was overjoyed at the retrieval of his goose and his father explained that it was the first grey he had ever shot.

Then I noticed that Meg was shivering violently. After removing my camouflaged waxproof, I took off my pullover and used the woollen garment to give her a good rub down. Sensing that all was not well with her, I told the father and son that I had better get her home as quickly as possible and took my leave of them. Because I was obliged to stop every now and then to allow Meg to catch up with me, it took quite a long time to reach the parking place and I had to lift the poor wee bitch bodily into the boot of the car. Snuggling down on top of my coat and gamebag she looked gratefully into my eyes and feebly wagged her tail.

As there was not much traffic on the roads I completed the journey in less than an hour but, when I arrived home and lifted the tailgate of the Volvo, I discovered that Meg was dead. She had passed away on a cold winter's morning within 90 minutes of retrieving her last goose.

That afternoon I returned to the estuary, travelling down the well-worn forest road to reach the sand dunes on the north shore. It was a place where, during her younger years, I had spent countless happy hours with Meg so I buried her on top of the highest dune at a spot which overlooked miles of wild foreshore. I then sat for a long, long time, staring out to sea and remembering the many wildfowling exploits which the faithful labrador had shared with me.

The richest of those memories were of days when she and I were alone on the marsh and, huddled together with our backs to a January storm, I had felt that we were a million miles from the civilised world. Those were times before she decided that her own instincts were more reliable than my commands. Yet, looking back, I knew that those instincts invariably led to a successful retrieve even if I had doubts as to whether a bird had actually been hit.

I appreciated then that a chapter in my wildfowling career had drawn to a close and, although Moy was to give many more years of loyal service and other dogs would capture my affection, I have never since experienced the unbelievable degree of true comradeship which Meg provided so consistently during those pre-dawn hours on a dark estuary. She was a labrador who shared the very spirit of fowling.

Just as many wildfowling adventures are rendered memorable by the dogs which featured in them, so too can others be readily recalled by virtue of the guns which contributed to their success or failure. There must be few fowlers who have not suffered, at some stage in their lives, from the affliction of "gunitis", a disease which affects the mind rather than the body and for which there is no cure other than painful experience. Most commonly the ailment stems from a desire to extend the range of one's armament so that those high-flying geese or duck might be brought tumbling from the heavens. I wonder how many devotees of the sport have had cause to look back and, with the benefit of hindsight, wish that they had kept faith with the very first shotguns they owned.

There are, of course, other reasons for shooting with a variety of guns. Many of us had no alternative but to set out in the sport armed with a handed-down gun or an inexpensive secondhand model. Perhaps, as our bank balances permitted, we would seek to upgrade to a better finished or more reliable weapon. Occasionally, too, the opportunity might arise to acquire a particularly interesting fowling piece or emulate the longshore gunners of yesteryear by shooting with a muzzle loader or large-bore hammer gun.

In my own case, all three causes played their respective parts in the passage of many different shotguns through my hands but, in retrospect, I fear that only a few of that veritable arsenal really earned their keep. Rapidly discarded were a Spanish sidelock which never really fitted me, a semi-automatic magnum which malfunctioned more often than not, an over-and-under from Japan which kicked like a mule and a 3-shot 10-bore which, although very effective, cost a small fortune to feed with expensive ammunition. Despite those failures, there have been one or two guns which carry memories of excellent service or which, in themselves, were of such intrinsic interest as to warrant mention.

One morning, not long before that day when Meg, Moy and Foss all turned white with frost, Leon and I had been shooting on the estuary and my performance with the ill-fitting Spanish sidelock had been so poor that I came off the shore completely scunnered with the gun. Without even stopping to clean the condemned weapon, we drove into the city and sat outside a gunshop waiting for it to open. Right on the stroke of 9 o'clock the owner arrived and, as soon as the front door was unlocked, he had a customer enquiring about a trade-in. I must have handled most of the shotguns in the shop, including many which were well out of my price range, before selecting a beautifully finished over-and-under by Beretta of Italy.

That very afternoon, with the new gun carefully protected in a padded slip, I went to the smaller estuary in the hope of seeing some duck. Arriving earlier than necessary, some time was spent in rebuilding a cairn of stones which, years before, an enterprising fowler had erected to give a modicum of cover on an otherwise featureless shore. With that task completed, I crouched down behind my artificial hide to await dusk.

As daylight slowly faded some shelduck took to the air and circled confidently over the inner basin before re-alighting on an area of mud which had been newly uncovered by the ebbing tide. Little parties of redshank flew upriver, their shrill piping carrying clearly in the still air. I hurriedly removed the No.6 cartridges from the pristine chambers of my new gun and replaced them with No.3's when the sound of pinkfeet descended upon the foreshore. For a minute I scanned the far horizon for the source of the goose music but, as the wavering skein finally came into view, I saw that the pinks were about 300 yards high. They did not lose height until well out over the sands and it was pleasing to note an absence of gunfire, signifying that no wayward gunner had dug-in on their roost.

Placing the lighter loaded cartridges back in the gun, I had to wait another 30 minutes or so before any duck flighted within range but, when they did, it was in classic style. First of all a spring of 13 or 14 teal zipped overhead and, so sudden was their appearance, there was time for only a single shot before they passed by. Moy had no sooner retrieved the fallen cock when three mallard came low over the mud, a single duck leading two drakes. The Beretta barked twice and the female and one drake fell to the ground. A few more mallard flighted inland but none of those ventured sufficiently close to draw a shot then, just as the last light began to fail, a solitary whistle attracted my attention. Glancing over my left shoulder I was almost too late for the group of four wigeon which sped past in the wrong direction but, throwing the over-and-under up and squeezing the trigger once, I was mildly surprised to see the hindmost bird collapse and drop to the mud.

On and on they came, their progress slowed by the wind, until they appeared to be motionless in the sky 40 yards above my hiding place. I pulled back the huge hammer of the 4-bore, rose to my feet and swung the long damascus barrel through the body, neck and head of the leading bird. Then everything seemed to happen in slow motion.

As the trigger was pulled I distinctly heard the fall of the hammer on the striking pin, was aware of a cruel thump against my shoulder, tried to take a step backwards to keep my balance but, with feet stuck in the soft mud, failed to do so. The pall of black powder smoke was carried away in the gale and, as I slowly fell backwards, I saw the goose tumble from the sky.

With the pinkfoot safely retrieved and the worst of the mud wiped from my hands, I placed the precious spent cartridge case in my pocket and reloaded the gun but, although I waited for another hour, no more geese came near.

The other gun which Patrick placed in my temporary custody was a double-barrelled 8-bore manufactured by J & W Tolley. This piece had two folding leaf sights fitted to the rib of its 34" brown barrels, suggesting that it started life as a double elephant rifle and had later been bored out to serve as a wildfowling gun. After my experience with the 4-bore, I decided to try the Tolley on the clay pigeon range before taking it out to the geese. Fortunately, I discovered that the weight of the gun was sufficient to absorb the recoil and it was as comfortable to shoot as any normal shotgun.

With my initial stock of cartridges expended on the clays, I then had to track down some more and, following a lead from a notice in the window of a deserted shop in Auchterarder, found the redoubtable Alex Kerr proudly installed in new premises in Crieff. Alex has long been famed for pandering to the needs of shooting men and had hand-loaded a stock of Eley 8-bore cases so, after parting with œ7.50, I left his shop clutching 10 new shells neatly wrapped in a brown paper bag. Why waste money on fancy cardboard cartons?

To give the Tolley hammer gun a fair trial, I took it for a morning flight at the Big Loch. There were rumoured to be 9,000 geese in residence so, although I had access to only a few hundred yards of its 12 mile shoreline, it was a reasonable bet that one or two might come my way.

At the farm gate I found that Peter and Henry were also out that morning and they took great interest in the 8-bore. I tried to explain that its range was not much greater than that of a 12-bore but, secretly, I hoped that its extra firepower might pay dividends if the pinkfeet were on the tall side.

The two young lads selected positions near the boundary burn in the hope of getting a few shots at duck before the geese came off. Their plan was rewarded and, from my own hide 50 yards along the reed beds, I saw a mallard pay the price for flying too low on its journey back to the loch from the autumn stubbles. When the pinks did flight, they came from the far side of the expansive water and skein after skein passed over well out of range.

Just as a few days earlier it had been latecomers which gave the 4-bore a chance to prove its worth so, that morning, the main flight was over before a group of 5 geese approached at a respectable height. Pulling back both hammers, I sank lower into the reeds and watched them come. The birds were just about 45 yards high so, with total confidence, I sprang up, swung through the first goose and pulled the front trigger. Swinging on to another bird I let the second 2-ounce load of shot fly on its deadly course. As the deep resonant bass notes of the 8-bore died away, I watched with disbelief as all 5 pinkfeet wheeled to the left and carried on flying. Then there was one sharp crack from Peter's game gun and a goose fell to the ground.

Which only goes to confirm that heavy shot charges are of no benefit at all if the gun is not pointing in the right direction. The Tolley was later to earn its pay but more than a fortnight had elapsed and my stock of ammunition was almost exhausted before I found the place with it. Nevertheless, there was something really special about the experience of using those great fowling pieces. Relics from the annals of bygone times they might have been but shooting with them provided just a glimpse back into the days when hardy professional fowlers would risk starvation if they failed to make every shot count. A tabloid gossip columnist once described Patrick Keen as a "wealthy eccentric" - it was to my eternal regret that he was not sufficiently eccentric to forget to request the return of his beautiful guns!

Chapter 6

American Adventures

So far, this story has had a perfectly ordinary beginning. It has been the tale of a perfectly ordinary wildfowler based in east-central Scotland. Then, by one of those extraordinary co-incidences, a chance encounter occurred that was to take the wildfowler to distant places where he would experience the very cream of fowling and meet some of the world's keenest waterfowl hunters

To cut a long tale short, my wife and I were amongst the lucky ones to benefit from Hoover's "Free Flights" offer back in 1993. Courtesy of the carpet-sweeper company, we found ourselves flying from the UK to Orlando, Florida whereupon we rented a car and set out for a two-week tour of the Southern States of the USA.

On that vacation we visited Georgia, South Carolina, North Carolina, Tennessee, Alabama, Mississippi and Louisiana but, for the purposes of this story we need only be concerned with our short stay in Charleston, S.C.

After booking into a motel in Mount Pleasant, we drove into the city centre and sought out the Charleston Visitor Centre to find out what there might be to see and do in that city. On arrival at the Visitor Centre we discovered that the car park was closed due to construction work and we had to drive around the block to find a parking space in a back street. Fortunately we found a vacant meter in King Street - right outside a shop front which bore the legend "South Carolina Waterfowl Association".

In we went - and were made very welcome by the staff. Coffee and chat took up longer than expected but it was a great way to spend an afternoon. Anyway, after we returned to the UK I received a phone call from the Director of the SCWA explaining that their big fundraiser each year was a Sportsman's Banquet each February at which they had an auction. Might I, he wondered, be able to host a week's "hunting" in Scotland for two of their members as an auction item? In return, they would be happy to reciprocate by hosting a week shooting waterfowl and deer in South Carolina for myself and a friend.

That was how it started and it has led directly to a series of adventures that was to span several years. See what I mean about chance co-incidences? If that car park at the Charleston Visitor Centre had not been dug up, none of this would have happened. Read on:

South Carolina was where it all really started. David Wielicki, the Director of the South Carolina Waterfowl Association, set up a wonderful programme for us - partly based at the SCWA Waterfowl and Wetlands Centre and partly at the homes of several of his association's members.

Having already hosted the first leg of the exchange scheme in Scotland earlier in the season, Tony Conroy and I arrived at Charlotte airport in December 1995 after an eventful journey. Our flight from Edinburgh to Gatwick had been diverted to Heathrow due to fog and we had to race by transfer bus to catch our plane to the USA. We made it - but our luggage and shotguns did not! Not to worry. We borrowed 20-bores for the first afternoon's quail hunt and our own guns arrived in time for the evening duck flight.

That first day's shooting was provided by Bob Stuck who was initiating a mallard release programme using wild-stock ducks brought down from Wisconsin. For many years mallard had been in short supply in the southern states and a scientifically monitored release programme was seen as the only solution. (As a footnote, five years later, it is interesting to see just how successful this programme has been. Indeed, the Wisconsin mallard rearing operation has now been moved down to South Carolina.)

Because of an exceptionally strange American rule that all duck shooting must be finished half an hour after sunset, we had the unaccustomed experience of decoying mallard into the marshes in daylight. Frankly, the ducks did not seem to mind and we had great sport despite having to pack up just about the time that we would have been starting at home. Most of the ducks on this shoot were mallard but Tony achieved the distinction of shooting a wood duck that afternoon.

That night we travelled with David Wielicki down to the SCWA Centre and what an incredibly impressive place it turned out to be. The achievements of the SCWA really put the efforts of shooting and conservation organisations in the UK to shame. Hundreds of acres of former clay mines had been restored to provide a very wide range of wetlands habitat and a conference centre with residential accommodation had been provided on a grand scale.

Here we experienced many of the features of American waterfowling that really differentiate it from British wildfowling. Hides (or blinds as the Americans call them) are constructed with a great deal of care, large decoy spreads are commonplace and fowlers have really worked hard to perfect their duck-calling skills. And, of course, such dedication and careful preparation really pay off. With goodness-knows how many million duck hunters in the USA, hunting pressure in some areas is heavy and the ducks become far wilder and warier than we find on the coastal marshes of Britain. If I had previously put the obsession with calls and decoys in the US down to affectation, I now had to revise that opinion. Without such finely-tuned skills, the American waterfowler would go home with an empty bag.

The shoot at the waterfowl centre was one of a series of regular events planned for members. The following morning, however, we experienced something more akin to British wildfowling. One of the association's biologists took us out for a dawn flight on Lake Marion. This is a very large freshwater lake that, for the most part, is only a few feet deep. There is a lot of flooded timber around the margins and a huge number of reed banks, both at the edges and in the middle.

Finding cover was no problem at all. We simply jumped out the john-boat at a likely looking clump of reeds and waited for the flight to begin. Once again it was Tony who got the less common specie - a gadwall this time.

The remainder of our week was spent visiting the private shoots of a number of SCWA members. Those that really stick in the memory are the duck shoots of Johnny Evans and Al Bullington - the latter being the farm on which I shot my first whitetailed deer. For sheer cussedness, however, the prize must go to the shoot run by Jimmy Hills on a reclaimed rice plantation not very far from the Santee Delta.

Jimmy's cabin is, in itself, an amazing place. A tattered Confederate flag adorns the veranda - along with a huge quantity of duck decoys and buck racks. Jimmy is one of the prime movers of the SCWA wood duck nesting box programme and his plantation is a perfect example of wood duck territory. It was, therefore, with keen anticipation that we prepared for a morning flight out on his marsh.

Tony and I were given careful instructions about where to find cover on the marsh (we were assured that the alligators would be hibernating!) and told that we must not shoot before the official time of 30 minutes before sunrise. Having found our places, we waited for the appointed hour. As we stood, up to our waists in South Carolinian marsh, the wood duck simply poured our from the flooded timber surrounding our positions. For perhaps 20 minutes there was a constant stream of ducks passing over our heads within easy range.

Then, exactly 90 seconds before shooting time, the flow stopped. Tony and I confirmed with each other that the critical moment had arrived - but despite waiting in place for another half hour, not a single wood duck came by. Jimmy's only explanation was that the ducks had invested in some new quartz watches and that the game warden had educated them about shooting times!

The only wildfowling that I had previously done in North America was with Tom Kennedy in Nova Scotia and that had been essentially similar to the type of shooting we do in Scotland. This experience in South Carolina, in contrast, was totally different in almost every respect. The novelty of the sport and the warmth of our hosts made it a week that will never be forgotten.

The year after the South Carolina trip, it was decided to continue the sporting exchange scheme. That year David Wielicki suggested that Tony and I might prefer to spend a week in October at the cottage owned by his father at Delta Beach in Manitoba. The Canadian waterfowl season opens earlier than in the USA and Manitoba hosts huge numbers of migrating ducks and geese during the early part of the season. In fact, that year was to be the first of three consecutive years that we visited Delta, so let me roll them into one account as the key elements of each were essentially similar.

Delta Beach is the ideal base for waterfowling in Manitoba. It is located less than 90 minutes drive from Winnipeg airport and is right on the famous Delta Marshes. Apart from the wetlands of the marshes themselves, there are many excellent fowling opportunities on the shores of Lake Manitoba and there is a wealth of farmland which attracts hundreds of thousands of snow geese.

A few hundred yards from the Wielicki cottage was the entrance to the West Marsh which is located just across the road from the wildfowl sanctuary surrounding the world-renowned Delta Waterfowl Research Station. Each time we shot this marsh we would take the quad bike (what the Americans call a "four-wheeler") through a mile of dense reed beds to reach the edge of open water. From there, canoes were used to ferry guns and decoys out to the North Point. In situations like this no hides are required as the phragmytes and cat-tails give adequate cover if one is well camouflaged. The Americans and Canadians are, of course, experts at camouflage - in addition to camouflaged jackets, trousers, hats and gloves, even their chest waders are in camouflage neoprene! The favoured pattern is Mossy Oak "Shadow Grass" and I have subsequently found that this is an ideal camouflage pattern for wildfowling in Britain.

Especially if there is a strong north wind, the North Point of the West Marsh can be an excellent place to draw all sorts of ducks into the decoy spread. One morning towards the end of our first week at Delta the weather changed overnight and everything was frozen solid by dawn. David and his father opted to break ice to get a canoe to the North Point but Tony and I, being less confident at canoeing, decided to remain on the shore at the end of the four-wheeler trail. Needless to say, we chittered with cold and fired hardly a shot while David and his Dad both shot limits of mallard drakes.

One morning during our second year at Delta we rose long before dawn, took the four-wheeler through the reed beds, canoed over to the North Point, spread out a few dozen decoys and got into position. Tony then remembered that it was his wedding anniversary and that, with the 6 hour time difference between Manitoba and the UK, he should be phoning his wife that morning before she left home for work. So David's Dad had to canoe Tony back ashore, drive him back to the cottage in the four-wheeler and let him use the phone. By the time that they got back to the marsh, it had been my day for limiting-out on drake mallards.

This practice of being very selective about what one shoots is a fun way of spinning out a limit. There was one day that David, his friend Hank and I drove up to the west shore of Lake Manitoba and then canoed another mile or so from the road-end to a reed-fringed section of shoreline just over the "sea wall" from a DU marsh. I say "sea wall" because Lake Manitoba covers an area about half the size of Scotland and it is easy to imagine that it is an inland sea. We put out a few dozen dabbling duck decoys close to the shore, a few dozen divers a little farther out and, just for good measure, some goose decoys a few yards farther away.

All day long there were ducks of many species - mallard, teal, American wigeon, greater and lesser scaup, pintail, shoveler, redhead, canvasback, goldeneye, bufflehead, etc. - dropping in to the decoy spread. To avoid shooting our limits in the first hour, we decided that only one of us would shoot at each flight of ducks that came in and that we would shoot only drake mallard or canvasback. Anyone shooting a hen of those two species, or either sex of any other variety of duck, would miss their next turn. Games like this certainly hone one's wildfowl identification skills!

Concepts such as bag limits and time limits may seem anathema to the British fowler but they do help to moderate the sport and North American waterfowlers seem to accept them quite readily. There was one day when the time limit thing was really frustrating, however. In 1997 the first two weeks in October had a rule that limited goose shooting to the mornings. Having decoyed geese at dawn on some corn stubbles, without a great deal of success, we decided to hunt ducks in the afternoon at Dinwiddie Marsh, a small marsh about 10 miles from Delta. There was a gale blowing from the south-west and the geese returning to feed on the fields after their mid-day siesta were struggling against the wind. Their flightline passed right over Dinwiddie Marsh and it is no exaggeration to say that, for 3 hours, there was a constant stream of snow geese over our positions - none of them more than 30 yards high. We must have had several thousand geese within range of our guns that afternoon but we daren't pull a trigger.

There was a similar experience that year on a harvested pea field. We had seen tens of thousands of ducks spiralling down to feed on this field - one of those rare occasions when the fowl literally do "blacken the sky". We sought permission from the farmer to shoot there the following afternoon and, not only was permission granted, but we were advised that there were two pit-blinds dug in the centre of the field. Next day we went out after lunch and set a decoy spread around the pits and waited for the ducks to come. Well, let me tell you, there may have been 20,000 - 30,000 ducks wanting to come into that field but they were very decoy-shy and our shooting was pretty sporadic. Then, after a couple of hours, the Canada geese started to move off the lake and several parties of them pitched right amongst our decoys without hesitation. Of course, by then, it was past noon and we couldn't shoot them.

All in all, the Delta Marsh area of Manitoba is a fantastic place to go duck and goose hunting. No two years were the same but the hospitality was always first class. Tony Wielicki always kept us entertained with his incredible sense of humour. Darla and Garry Sanderson were typical of the Manitoba farming community who made us so very welcome on their farmland. Joyce, Joe and Suzanne fed us huge breakfasts, at any time of the day, at their great little restaurant. They also sold hunting permits!

In 1999 we departed from the usual exchange arrangement and accepted an invitation from Bob Stuck and Tim Brown to join them on a trip to Mistik Lodge on the Cumberland Marsh in northern Saskatchewan. This trip would not only introduce us to a new venue but also give Tony and me the opportunity to meet up again with some of our other friends from South Carolina like Jimmy Hills and Al Bullington.

So, in mid-September, we flew to Winnipeg and joined up with the South Carolina party. Bob had his Beechcraft King Air twin turbo-prop while Tim was flying his new Cessna Citation jet. Flying those aircraft, it was only another 90 minutes before we had landed at the gravel airstrip at Cumberland House and transferred to fast boats for the last leg of the journey to Mistik Lodge.

Mistik Lodge itself is located on the banks of the North Saskatchewan River in the heart of the Cumberland House Delta and is on the edge of a marsh that extends to an area almost 100 miles by 30 miles. At this time of year, the marsh holds about 10 million ducks, principally mallard, pintail, greenwing teal, bluewing teal, American wigeon, shoveler and gadwall. The Lodge is run by Gary Carriere who, like his staff of guides and housekeepers, is a Cree Indian with an immense knowledge of the area and it wildlife.

The Lodge has a main cabin with lounge, dining and kitchen facilities and there are three 4-person cabins for guests. The food was absolutely amazing - both in quality and quantity! Because much of the marsh is too shallow to navigate by boats, the Lodge uses three airboats (Florida Everglades style) to take hunters out to meet the ducks. Garry has perfected a portable blind arrangement consisting of a galvanised frame that sits in the marsh. A plywood floor is placed on the frame and a padded swivel seat and a cartridge tray are fitted to stems welded to the frame. Using those devices, a two-person hide can be constructed in the reeds in a matter of minutes.

A typical day at the Lodge would involve being awakened by the cabin stove being stoked by Walter the odd-job man at 4.30 a.m., after which a quick snack would be consumed while discussing the morning's plans. Two pairs of hunters per airboat would then set out and each pair would be dropped off at a prime location where the guide would build a two-person hide, set out the decoys and then depart in the airboat to do the same for the other pair. Sunrise at such a northerly latitude was always spectacular and, before long, the ducks would be trading back and forward across the marsh. Mallard and pintail often required to be called to attract their attention to the decoys but wigeon and teal frequently arrived unannounced and the first we would see of them would be the realisation that some additional fowl were swimming amongst the decoys.

Morning flight would usually last about 3½ hours and then the airboat would return, the guide would pick up the shot ducks, retrieve the decoys and dismantle the platforms and seats. Back at the Lodge a really hearty breakfast would be waiting (8 eggs, 4 pancakes, half a dozen sausages and several rashers of crispy bacon per hunter was just for starters!). Stories from the morning flight would be swapped and some lesser mortals might decide to catch a nap or consume a crate of Bud while breakfast settled. For the more active, there could be a choice of going fishing for walleye and northern pike or trying to walk-up some sharptailed grouse to pass a few hours before it was time for evening flight. Even moose hunting with a bow and arrow was on the agenda for those so inclined.

Evening flight followed the same pattern as morning flight but the intensity tended to increase as darkness fell. We had one really spectacular evening when I was sharing a hide with Al Bullington. We were hidden in a clump of reeds close to the edge of the "Big Water" - several thousand acres that, had it been more than a few inches deep, would have been classified as a lake - and we had a constant influx of mallard and wigeon for the better part of three hours. Latterly we simply stopped shooting and had a great time competing to see whose calling skills were most acceptable to the fowl.

At night, back in camp, there was a great deal of story-telling, liquor-consuming and joke-relating. Dinner was always a massive and leisurely affair and, on clear nights, we could marvel at the Northern Lights dancing across the sky. Being hundreds of miles from the nearest street lights resulted in the sky being inky-black and the stars shining with an intensity never seen in Britain.

One highlight of the trip was having a duck "stolen" by a Golden Eagle. It was a morning flight and the sunrise had been especially brilliant (in fact, the photo on the Front Page of this website was taken that morning). I was sharing a hide with Tony and we had been shooting well for a couple of hours. Although there was no current in the water at that part of the marsh, there was a strong westerly wind and the dead ducks which had fallen into the water around our hide gradually drifted eastwards in the wind. before long, we had a "litter" of ducks spread out from the hide for a distance of two or three hundred yards downwind. Once the sun was fairly high in the sky, a golden eagle started surveying our section of marsh and the sound of gunshots did not seem to worry it at all. It made several passes over our ribbon of floating ducks before stooping down magnificently and picking a shot mallard from the water in its talons.

We really could not grudge such a noble bird an easy breakfast. There were also Bald Eagles seen over the marsh from time to time but they lack the splendour and grace of the larger Golden. It did occur to me to think how typically American it was for the USA to adopt the Bald Eagle - a scavenging carrion eater more akin to a vulture than a real eagle - as its "national" bird when they could have opted for the infinitely superior Golden Eagle. Such masters of the art of understatement are the Yanks! (Just joking!)

As always happens, our week was over far too quickly but we will never forget the time spent wildfowling with the Cree Indians at Mistik Lodge.

Epilogue

The sport of wildfowling has a long and noble past, having captured the enthusiasm and imagination of mankind since earliest times. Long before the invention of firearms, the value of duck and geese as both food source and sporting quarry was recognised throughout the world. Chinese, Egyptian and Roman artefacts dating back to 1300BC bear witness to the ingenuity which our predecessors brought to the pursuit, utilising throwing sticks, bows, clap nets and decoys to cull a harvest of fowl from the marshes. Early in the 17th century the development of relatively reliable flintlock guns made wing shooting a practicable proposition and, by the time a further 100 years had passed, the origins of fowling as we know it today were well established. Each improvement in shotgun design increased the efficiency with which the wildfowler could pursue his quarry until, with the advent of the hammerless breech-loader and modern nitro powders, the optimum weaponry became available to the longshore gunner.

Having moved into the 21st Century, wildfowling is in good heart but exponents of the craft cannot afford the luxury of being complacent about the future. Wildfowl populations and habitats require to be conserved, political threats to traditional countryside activities have to be tackled and fowlers must constantly reappraise the manner in which the essential freedoms of their sport can be accommodated within a society which is subject to ever-increasing regulation.

In the vanishing landscape of the British countryside the twin pressures of intensive agricultural and industrial development have eaten up vast tracts of marsh and fen which once harboured great hordes of wildfowl. In other countries, also, prime duck and goose habitat has disappeared or been threatened in a similar manner. Wildfowlers were not slow to recognise the dangers nor hesitant to meet the challenges presented by the changing rural scene. Led by WAGBI (now the British Association for Shooting & Conservation), many fowling clubs and dedicated individual sportsmen readily accepted the need to co-operate with other conservationists and the value of such joint initiatives was acknowledged in a booklet entitled

Wildfowl Conservation in Great Britain - The Story of a Triumvirate published by WAGBI, the Nature Conservancy and the Wildfowl Trust in 1970. More than 30 years later, we desperately need to rekindle that enthusiastic co-operation.

Conservation implies the management of limited or vulnerable resources in a way which will ensure their maintenance and increase. From the point of view of the wildfowler it makes a great deal of sense to offer sufficient protection to the wild populations of geese and duck to ensure that their numbers are maintained despite the many adverse factors, such as habitat erosion, which are at work. To this end, a national network of wildfowl refuges was welcomed, many wildfowling clubs established their own wildfowl sanctuary zones and fowling interests became represented on the management committees of important nature reserves.

In the years ahead it will become increasingly necessary for wildfowlers to demonstrate their commitment to reserve areas. Only when sanctuary zones are managed, directly or indirectly, by wildfowling clubs and organisations can we be confident that the future of the sport is secure. The alternative is an escalation of land purchase and reserve creation by protectionist bodies which may not always be sympathetic to shooting. Already there are tragic examples of marshes which, for many years, were exceedingly well managed by wildfowling clubs being bought by protectionist organisations and all shooting proscribed. In some parts of the country well-organised fowling clubs have countered this threat by purchasing the freehold of the areas which traditionally they have shot but much greater financial resources will be required if this trend is to continue. The BASC's Wildlife Habitat Trust Fund has a very important part to play in this process.

There is still a great deal which is not fully understood about the behaviour of wildfowl, the effects of habitat changes upon their distribution, the manner in which breeding success influences long-term population levels and many similar matters. In order that wildfowlers may contribute to the overall stock of knowledge concerning their quarry and, more particularly, that scientifically derived evidence may be available to repulse any threat to the sport, it is highly desirable that the BASC's research programme continues to expand.

Already much sterling work has been undertaken by the research staff at Marford Mill, with many clubs and individual wildfowlers playing a crucial role by collecting and supplying data to the research projects. It would be a tragedy if research of this nature was curtailed due to lack of support by wildfowlers. In the absence of properly conducted investigations there would be a great deal of additional scope for opponents of shooting sports to present fallacies and half-truths in support of their arguments.

One of the most important functions of the BASC is to monitor political activity at local authority, government and European levels. In many parts of the country the designation of Sites of Special Scientific Interest (SSSIs) and Special Protection Areas (SPAs) posed a threat to wildfowling which had to be countered. Any draft legislation affecting land use, wildlife conservation or firearms must be carefully studied and the appropriate representations made.

It is likely that, in future years, governments will come under increasing pressure from protectionist organisations, the law and order lobby and European directives to introduce or amend statutes in ways which would be detrimental to shooting sports. The only effective safeguard which wildfowlers have is a strong and influential parent body and it is not too severe to suggest that, in Britain today, no person deserves to carry a shotgun unless he also carries a BASC membership card in his pocket.

Much of the political antipathy to country sports is founded upon ignorance and an absence of rational thought. A very high proportion of the population lives in urban conurbations and has little knowledge or understanding of the ways of the countryside. Nurtured on the "cuddly bunny" syndrome, many people see the world of nature through rose-coloured spectacles which are often tinted to the point of opacity. They do not appreciate that there are only four ways in which a duck or goose can die - by predation, starvation, disease or shooting and that, in anybody's terms, shooting is the least unpleasant of those. To a countryman it may seem strange that the city dweller who decries fieldsports can quite happily go into a supermarket and buy a plastic-wrapped battery fowl for their family dinner but few of the people who oppose shooting stop to think in those terms.

Despite the irrationality of their arguments and actions, the animal liberation fanatics cannot be ignored. The fact that over five million people in Britain engage in fieldsports may convince all of the major political parties that it would be electoral suicide to legislate for the total abolition of shooting or fishing but there remains a danger that our sports will be eroded at the edges by restricting the quarry species or by imposing further regulations upon the possession and use of firearms. It is up to each and every wildfowler to maintain public relations of the highest standard in order to counteract the pressures of our opponents.

One of the most effective ways of avoiding unnecessary statutory restrictions upon wildfowling is to voluntarily accept sensible and moderate codes of conduct. Many of the traditions of fowling are founded upon the great sense of freedom which the estuarine gunner experiences when he is out on the saltings long before dawn. It is, therefore, understandably an anathema to many fowlers to suggest that they should accept a degree of regulation which would never have been dreamed of by their forefathers. The rise of wildfowling clubs was not universally popular nor, until recently, was the

BASC accepted by many shooters. Nevertheless, there can be few wildfowlers who do not now recognise that the state of their sport would be very much poorer today had it not been for the efforts of the BASC and its affiliated clubs during recent decades.

In some coastal areas the introduction of wildfowling permit schemes is still resented and any mention of bag limits is sure to arouse strong emotions where fowlers gather together. Compared to our contemporaries in the USA or in most European countries we still have a much-envied degree of freedom and there are aspects of this which we should cherish and carefully nurture. On the other hand, where a slight restriction on our practices can be shown to be to the long-term benefit of our sport or where a little modification to our traditional behaviour might secure a better future for our quarry, we should not automatically throw up our hands in horror. By being seen to be responsible, logical, well-informed and caring in our attitudes to the duck and geese of the marsh, we will ensure that our sons and grandsons may also enjoy that unique combination of solitude, tranquillity, excitement and fulfillment which is the heritage of every true wildfowler in Britain today.

The goose used in the chapter headings of this book is the Pinkfooted Goose (Anser branchyrhynchus), by far the most prized quarry species of British wildfowlers.

Printed in Poland
by Amazon Fulfillment
Poland Sp. z o.o., Wrocław